Winning Tactics for Weekend Tennis

# Winning Tactics for Weekend Tennis
Tony Trabert with Joe Hyams

Holt, Rinehart and Winston

New York   Chicago   San Francisco

To my wife, Emeryl, and my
children, Brooke and Mike,
who are destined to be
weekend players
and to Bill Talbert
who taught me doubles
in the first place

# CONTENTS

# INTRODUCTION

This book was written because so many week-end players have asked me to help them improve their doubles games. They rarely ask about particular strokes because their mechanics are already set. What they want is to make the most of what they already have. And that's what this book is all about—how to make the most of what you have.

The professional player won't find much in these pages that he doesn't already know, but the novice or weekend player will, because the questions I've answered are those that have been asked me hundreds of times during the ten years since I stopped playing tennis professionally.

I understand the problems of the weekend player who loves the game. I still play men's doubles and "hit and giggle" tennis several times a week for fun. Although I was a champion and have been playing tennis since I was six years old, I have had to accept the reality that eventually confronts all of us when we're over forty and overweight and our reflexes are a little slower.

I don't play the way I used to and I know it. There's nothing more boring than some fellow who used to play well and still thinks he plays as he did and makes all the alibis. The truth is that no man is as good at forty as he was at twenty-five. That's all there is to it and I don't care if he plays every day.

More than ever I recognize the importance of a proper warm-up. I've never had a so-called tennis elbow and I think the routine I follow has helped me avoid it. I may look like a big white polar bear out on the court as I warm up, but I don't start to peel off my clothing until I begin to perspire. After I finish playing, I bundle right back up and am careful not to stick my elbow out of the car window when I'm driving home or sit around in wet clothes.

I did all those things while I was in competition so I wouldn't hurt myself and could stay in good shape. Now I do them to avoid stiffness and soreness that comes from overextending myself when my muscles are less flexible.

We all change physiologically. The brain tells us what to do but the body doesn't react as quickly as it once did. We slow down, so we have to attempt shortcuts without affecting our productivity. We have to buy time and let our opponents defeat themselves whenever possible. We learn to use our heads more and our feet less.

And that's part of the great joy of doubles. It's a thinking man's game. The more you think the more aware you are of what is taking place on the court. If you have any kind of game plan, you will certainly be more effective even though everything you try undoubtedly will not work.

Doubles is not just singles with two players on each side of the net instead of one. Doubles is unity and teamwork. The better you and your partner know one another and the more often the two of you play together, the better you should play once you understand doubles and know what you're trying to achieve.

I take calculated risks, gambling only when the reward is big enough. And I try to avoid setting a pattern in my play.

I try to stay out of trouble by not hitting the ball in areas of my opponents' court which open up my own court for a return that forces me to really run. That's using strategy more and the legs less.

Statistics compiled after studying each point in hundreds of matches over a period of years indicate that the majority of points are not won by brilliant shots. Flashy players are not usually the winners. It's the fellow who keeps his level of consistency high who generally wins.

My game has changed over the years. I'm still competitive and I still like to win, but I have learned to simplify my movements, not just to conserve energy but to make up for the lack of speed and timing familiar to anyone who doesn't play every day.

Originally I had not planned to discuss mixed doubles, because in California where I live there's a theory that the woman who plays mixed doubles is just a pretty prop on the court. The Beverly Hills Galahads ride roughshod over their female partners and opponents and that kind of tennis ends up as a jousting match between the men.

That's not the way it should be, however, and more and more women are playing good tennis and getting into men's matches. They are coming into their own as adversaries and partners but, because they are women, their physical capabilities are different. That doesn't mean they're not as good as men, just different—and thank heavens for it.

Some of the things you read in this book may not work the first few times. Frankly, I would be surprised if they did. I can tell you how to do something properly, but if you won't concentrate enough to watch the ball, nothing will help you.

I can help you with strategy so that you get the ball set up for a put away, but if your mechanics from then on are wrong, that doesn't mean the strategy is wrong.

Just because you have a sound plan doesn't mean that you can go out on the court and execute it right away. The only way you can become a good or proficient player is to try the proper thing over and over again until the correct stroke or response is automatic and spontaneous.

It's human nature to revert to your old habits under pressure. You must erase them and convince yourself that what you're doing is right. Soon, without even thinking about it, the correct fundamentals will be grooved in your mind.

P.S. from Joe Hyams:

A word of warning. Don't try to do everything Tony Trabert suggests all at once. I did and my game fell apart for several weeks. I was in a slump and even talked of giving up the game until Tony asked me why I was playing.

"To get some exercise and have fun," I admitted. "But I also like to win occasionally."

"Are you using the Check Lists?" Tony asked me.

I realized I had been ignoring them, so the next time my serve was off, I went over the Check List and found I had been trying to ace my opponents with the first serve instead of just getting it in. I concentrated on getting the first serve in and, miraculously, got into rhythm and even started to hit a few aces.

The same thing happened on another day with my backhand return of a lefty's service. I went over the Check List in my mind and the problem was solved.

My game strategy has improved a hundredfold. At forty-six I'm playing better doubles and enjoying the game much more than I did when I was a teen-ager.

The book works. If it can work for me, I believe it will work for anyone.

Winning Tactics for Weekend Tennis

*Which racket is better for the average player, metal or wood?*

I know players who swear by metal rackets and others who swear at them. Wooden rackets inspire the same mixed emotions. It usually depends on how the player is hitting on a given day.

Generally speaking, I believe the average player tends to gain more than he loses by playing with a metal racket. A metal racket is easier to swing because it offers less wind resistance.

More important, a metal racket absorbs a lot of the shock that normally travels up the arm when a ball is mis-hit and that shock is what increases the likelihood of tennis elbow. For that reason don't get a metal racket that's too stiff. If you do, you lose the advantage you're trying to gain.

A metal racket is also a more durable piece of equipment. It won't warp and doesn't need to be kept in a racket press when not in use.

And if you play tennis seriously, it's possible to duplicate your favorite metal racket precisely because they are machinemade. It's almost impossible to get two wooden rackets with the same balance, same weight, and same shape on the grip.

If you're already playing with a wood racket and want to try metal, I suggest you allow yourself lots of time to try out the new racket. You can't really tell much from the first few ground strokes or serves. You must play with a racket enough for you to become accustomed to it.

I know a man who shows up on the court for his weekend tennis carrying one metal and one wooden racket. He doesn't play well with either, but they are his alibi. When his serve is off, he changes rackets. If he misses an overhead, he switches rackets. He's a racket freak and it doesn't matter whether the racket is metal or wood, he's still going to play the same way. But that doesn't stop him from believing the magic is in the racket. It's not. It's in the player.

### How do I choose the proper-weight racket?

Get help from someone who is knowledgeable. Some salesmen in sporting goods stores can suggest a proper weight for you from just a glance at your size and build.

If you're built like King Kong, there's no point in getting a light-weight racket that you're going to use like a fly swatter.

If you're average size and weight, you should probably choose a medium-weight racket—between thirteen and fourteen ounces strung.

### How should the racket be balanced?

It should be evenly balanced. When you pick up a racket, you can tell quickly whether it's head-heavy or handle-heavy.

Most players should avoid a racket that's heavy in the head because it's harder to manipulate. If it's too light in the head, it won't counteract the weight of the ball when you make contact.

*Is nylon better than gut for the average player?*

I feel nylon is better because most people can't tell the difference between it and gut. Nylon is less expensive. It will last longer and moisture doesn't hurt it but will destroy gut. Nylon is also better if you use a metal racket, because the racket itself is quite lively and the nylon will help give better control.

*Should I buy an expensive racket?*

Adequate rackets for children can be purchased for eight or ten dollars strung with nylon. But an adult starting out in tennis should probably spend a little more money because the more expensive rackets are made better and will last longer.

Also, and let's not kid about this, there's a whole status thing about rackets. Most pros endorse one or another brand of racket. My own "Tony Trabert Signature" is made by Wilson Sporting Goods.

*How tight should I have my racket strung?*

If you're going to play under fast conditions—a fast court on a hot day or in a high altitude—your racket should be strung extra tight.

In heavier conditions—clay courts or damp grass—your racket should be strung a bit more loosely.

The average player in normal conditions should have his racket strung between 55 and 60 pounds of tension.

*How should I choose the proper grip?*

Most people tend to select a racket with a grip that's too small for their hand.

When you find a racket that feels proper in your hand, you might hold it in the forehand grip and have someone try to twist the head of the racket. If it does not turn in your hand, you probably have the right size but if it turns easily, try a larger size. The larger grip you can use the better.

# Clothing

*Must I wear white clothing when I play tennis?*

It's traditional to wear white and it's also wise since tennis is usually played in sunny weather and white is cooler. But some players today wear pastel colors which are now even permitted at staid old Wimbledon, the seat of tradition.

Personally, I think white looks better on players and it's also the color of most tennis clothes and accesssories. I have recently seen some ladies playing in leotards and ballet-type skirts and men in blue denims. It was not attractive. If someone wants to be colorful or casual, I think that's fine but not on the tennis court.

*Do you recommend warm-up suits?*

Yes indeed. Your body needs to be warmed up properly and the older you get the less flexible or supple you are. Older people especially should wear enough clothing to help them start perspiring. When finished playing they should bundle up again to avoid a chill. When I see an older man come on the court in a T-shirt and shorts, I expect that the next day he is probably going to ask me why he has a stiff back or arm.

*Do you have any suggestions for the proper type of playing shoe?*

The main thing is to buy the proper size taking into allowance that you will be wearing heavy socks. The shoe should be substantial enough to give your foot a reasonable amount of support and it should have a solid type of sole.

When I put on my tennis shoes, I don't lace them up tight until I get to the court. Then I lace them up properly. By keeping them loose until I am ready to play, I haven't shut off any circulation in my feet before getting onto the court.

*What about socks?*

Many people like to wear two pairs of socks: a thin pair of wool or cotton with heavier wool over them. The thin socks should be worn closest to the feet so that the friction is between the two socks rather than the socks and the feet.

Avoid wrinkles in your socks when you put them on. I also suggest avoiding synthetics like orlon because they do not absorb perspiration as well as natural fibers such as wool or cotton.

If I haven't played for a while, I sometimes put

pieces of moleskin on the balls of my feet to avoid blisters.

# General

*What about wearing sunglasses when I play?*

Unless you have a vision problem, I don't think anyone should wear sunglasses when he plays. I don't think you see as well with them and they are just something extra to worry about.

If you're not going to wear sunglasses when you play, then don't wear them on your way to the court because it will take some time for your eyes to readjust to the change in light.

*Is it bad to eat just before I play?*

There's an old adage in sports that you are better off being a little hungry than a little too full.

Nevertheless, many people eat too much and too soon before going out to play and then they wonder why they can't get started or why they have cramps.

If you're playing for real, you ought to eat a good meal at least three or four hours before the match. Perhaps a steak and some vegetables, some jello or ice cream and some tea.

*How do you suggest overcoming pre-game tension?*

Expending some energy is one of the best ways. Do some quick exercises or something that stimulates you and that will help get rid of the tension. Don't walk on the court half asleep and tight as a drum.

## 2.
# THE WARM-UP

*What is the purpose of the warm-up?*

Literally to get your body warm and your muscles loosened up. Try to get a feel of the court, whether the bounce is fast or slow. Pay attention to the bounce of the ball and the background which may help or interfere with your vision. Try to become aware of existing conditions such as wind direction.

You should also study your opponent and discover his capabilities. Hit him some forehands and backhands when he's at the net. See if he likes to hit top spin or whether he chops. Study his style of play. You could spot some things right away that might help you later.

Don't be intimidated by someone who looks great warming up. Such opponents are frequently thinking more about looking good than in studying you. There's a saying in tennis: "He won the warm-up but I won the match."

If there's time before the match, I recommend that you do some knee bends or jog in place. It's always a good idea to bend your knees when picking up the first few balls so you get the stiffness out.

The secret of a good warm-up is to gradually increase the tempo of your playing and strokes. Start slowly, wearing your sweater. When you increase tempo and begin to break a sweat, take the sweater off. If you're perspiring, chances are your muscles are beginning to elongate and become supple.

# The Warm-Up

*What is the technique of warming up properly?*

Start hitting from the position you would normally be playing: one step behind the baseline when hitting a forehand and backhand and halfway between the service line and the net when volleying. Don't stand too far behind the baseline when warming up. Practice from the normal playing position.

*Should I hit the ball harder or at normal pace when warming up?*

At normal pace. You are trying to simulate playing conditions. When I start warming up, I hit the ball fairly easy the first few times to get the feel of it and get loosened up and then I increase the tempo a little bit. But you shouldn't increase the tempo beyond that which you would normally use when playing.

*What is the best procedure to follow when the warm-up time is brief?*

Hit ground strokes so that you can get used to the speed of the court. Work on your ground strokes as much as possible and don't concern yourself with volleying; the ball travels through the air at the same speed anywhere, except in altitude. It's the speed of the court which is different.

When I go out to warm up, I don't chase the first few balls that are wide or otherwise difficult to return because I don't want to stretch my muscles when I'm still cold.

*What is meant by a "fast" or a "slow" court?*

The coarser the surface the slower the court is going to be. In effect there's more friction to hold on to the ball on a rough court.

The fastest court you can play on is varnished wood because the ball skids like a bullet. There are many different speeds of cement courts, depending on how rough the top surface is. Macadam- and asphalt-type courts are rough, so they are usually a little slower. Grass is fairly fast and a ball that has been hit hard is likely to scoot low over the grass after bouncing.

When I played pro tours, we used to take a canvas court around with us. The speed of the court then depended on what was underneath it. The fastest surface under the canvas was cement. When the canvas was laid on wood it was a little slower.

The best playing surface was over ice because the canvas adhered to the ice and the colder temperature slowed the ball down.

*How do we determine who is to play the ad or deuce court?*

The general rule is for the weaker player to be in the forehand court and the stronger in the backhand court, because it is usually thought that the stronger player should be the anchor man in the ad court. If the weaker player loses his deuce point, then the stronger man is more likely to get it back to deuce. My feeling is that it doesn't matter. I feel that the choice of who plays where depends on the strengths and weaknesses of each partner. Some players block their backhand service return and will normally be late in hitting, which means they might play better in the deuce court. Other players use a Continental forehand grip, which enables them to "hook" the ball cross court more easily. Ability with this shot might make them better in the deuce court.

Also, one player may handle the net better from one side or the other.

*If my partner is a left-hander and we are playing against a left-hander, is it better for my partner to play the ad or deuce court?*

Generally speaking it's better for your left-handed partner to play the ad court, because serves from the opposing left-hander will break wide to his forehand. However, if he plays the deuce court, both of you will have forehands to use for shots up the middle.

*Should I practice serves during the warm-up?*

Yes. The rule is that everyone should practice his serves prior to starting the match. Many people are in the habit of playing "the first good serve," which I think is wrong. Why not play "the first good return"?

The rules state that everybody warms up for a period of time and then the set starts. Everything from then on counts according to the rules of tennis.

*If my partner is unable to hit a forehand cross-court service return from the deuce court where should he play?*

Put him in the ad court. He is either slicing the ball or is too late hitting it, which means that he may be able to make an ideal forehand return from the ad court. This kind of situation dictates which partner should play which side of the court.

*I have to play at least a set before I get really warmed up. Is there anything I can do to speed the warming-up process?*

If it's an important match, you should arrange to warm up before you play. If you can't do that, then at least try to do some calisthenics. If you are able to gradually increase the pace of your shots, it may discourage your opponents.

In any event, you should dress warmly until you begin to perspire and your muscles loosen up.

*Should I play cautiously until I am warmed up?*

When you're cold and not acclimated it's a good idea to keep the ball down the middle of the court and in play but don't try the tough shots. For example, don't take the first serve that comes to your backhand in the ad court and try to hit it down the line if it's easier and more natural for you to hit cross court.

*What are the advantages and disadvantages of serving or receiving first?*

When I went out to play the finals at Wimbledon, I spun the racket and lost the toss. I didn't think I was in trouble if my opponents elected to serve first. That means the server is going to have to serve when he's not quite warmed up or adjusted to playing.

There are, however, certain psychological ramifications to consider. If your opponent serves first, it means that you will always be serving to catch up, which may give him a psychological advantage and put you at a disadvantage.

You will always be serving from behind if you hold serve and that may inflict some pressure on you if you are one of those people who prefer to be serving at four all, so if you lose service you have one more chance at winning your opponent's next serve.

It never bothered me a bit to be serving from behind, because no one has ever been able to dishearten me on a tennis court. I've been down one-five and said to myself, "If he can get to five-one and break my serve twice, then, why can't I break him twice and get to five all?" There's no position in tennis that your opponents can reach that you can't reach.

*I serve from the center stripe when playing singles. Is that a good position for serving in doubles?*

No, because when you run to your ideal position at net, you are going at an angle away from the most likely direction of the service return. It's better to serve from the center of the area which you must cover.

If you serve from the center stripe, you cannot slice a serve as wide in the deuce court, nor can you hit a serve as wide to the backhand in the ad court.

*Where should I stand?*

The basic technique of doubles is to divide responsibility for coverage of the court between you and your partner. At the same time you are trying to divide your opponent's possibilities in half.

When you are serving you should stand halfway between the singles sideline and the center of the court. That way you are in the center of the area which is your responsibility and you can rush to the net in a direct line to handle the service return.

*Is it all right if I stand nearer to the sideline?*

If you stand too wide it is almost physically impossible for you to serve the ball down the center of the service court and hurt your opponent. You also indicate to the receiver that your serve will

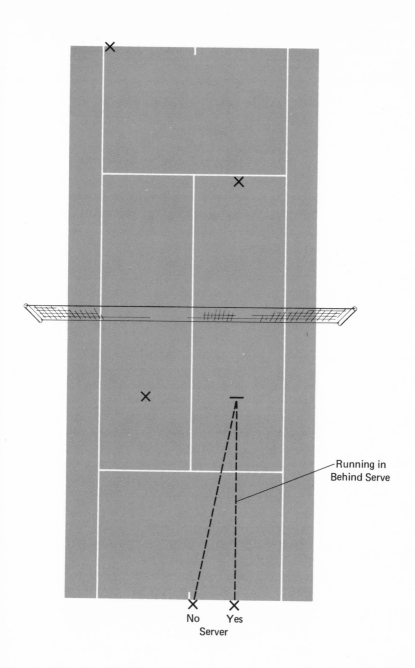

Running in
Behind Serve

No        Yes
Server

probably be wide and he will be able to prepare for it.

*What is the purpose of rushing to the net after serving?*

The theory of going to the net after the serve is that you force your opponents to try to hit a good shot. When you are at the net with your partner, you are in an offensive position and can pick off your opponents' shots and place the ball so it is difficult for them to return.

When all four of you are at the net, you should try to hit the ball low in relationship to the top of the net so when your opponents return the ball, they must lift it up, enabling you to contact the ball higher than the net and hit it down at them.

*Are there any tips for aiming a serve?*

I don't believe there is any specific tip for helping a server place the ball where he wants it to land. Some people look at the spot they are aiming for, forgetting that they have to look up in the air when they toss the ball to serve.

Other players point their feet in the direction they want to serve, but I think that's a habit rather than a technique of aiming.

I keep my feet in the same position regardless of where I am going to hit the service because I direct the ball with the wrist at impact. That way I don't telegraph my intentions.

Some players who slice their serve forget to

allow for the curve of the ball after it has left their racket. They start the ball at the spot they want it to land, ignoring the fact that it curves several feet in the air.

If you are serving to the deuce court and want to hit the ball near the center service line, start the serve to the right of the center service line, allowing for the curve. It's the opposite if you are a lefty.

*Where is the best place for me to aim my first serve?*

Most of the time it is better to serve straight at your opponent because that lessens the angle of his return. Also, it adds another problem for him. He must get his body out of the way to make the return.

If you serve to his right or left where he can reach the ball easily, all he has to do is turn and make his shot.

*Should I try for an ace with my first serve?*

The secret of doubles is to get your first serve in as often as possible. Basically, all you want to do is start the point so why hit the first serve hard, probably miss it, and risk a double fault with your shaky second serve?

You have a psychological edge on your opponent with the first serve because he doesn't know where the ball is coming or how hard it will be hit or with what spin.

My feeling is that you will be more effective hitting the first serve with less speed but getting a greater percentage in.

I would prefer you try for the occasional ace when you're at 40–15 on your serve and not 30–40. I certainly don't think you should attempt an ace on the first point of the first game when you're not acclimated or warmed up.

*Should I wait to see if the first serve is in before running to the net?*

You should be moving toward the net as you hit the serve. If you toss the ball forward, you will be "falling" toward the net as you hit it. The reason many people don't get to the net quickly is that they toss the ball straight up or behind the baseline instead of in front of them when they serve. Thus they hit the ball first and then start running.

If you toss the ball in front of you so you are hitting and falling forward at the time of impact, your momentum should get you near the service line in time to make your first volley.

*Why is it that I frequently get nailed by a ball at my waist or feet as I am rushing the net?*

If you watch any good tennis player you will see him run toward the net until his opponent is about to make a shot. Then he stops, takes a little jump and straddles in the ready position prepared to play wherever he is at that moment. He makes his volley and then moves forward again into the desired position.

You should never run into a ball that's landing in front of you. Stop, let it bounce, hit it, and then move forward. You should never hit a ball on the run unless there's no other way to get it.

There's another reason for coming to a complete stop. If you're running full speed ahead and I say to you, "Turn right," you're going to veer off at an angle to your right. The same thing happens if I say, "Turn left." What you have done in effect is make a "Y," because you have veered off in one way or another. But if you stop and then move to your right or left, you have made a "T." You go directly sideways to reach a ball and, consequently, you can cover the court better.

*Rule of thumb:* IF YOU'RE RUSHING THE NET YOU MUST COME TO A COMPLETE STOP AS YOUR OPPONENT IS ABOUT TO HIT THE BALL AND NOT AFTER HE HAS MADE CONTACT.

*What if I am unable to rush the net after serving?*

Any time you can't go to the net after your serve, you should instantly retreat one step behind the baseline to the position you would normally take when rallying.

*If I stay back after my serve, how can I get to the net?*

Stay behind the baseline until your opponents hit a short return. If one of your opponents re-remains near his baseline, hit the ball to him, going

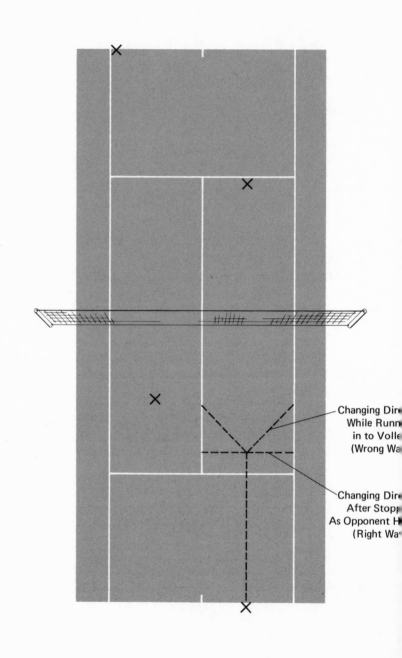

Changing Dir•
  While Runn•
  in to Volle
  (Wrong Wa

Changing Dir•
  After Stop•
As Opponent H•
  (Right Wa•

for depth rather than speed, and allowing yourself time to get to the net.

*Should I vary my serves?*

Yes, if you can do it without missing too many first serves. Some people have the notion that mixing their serves up is simply serving once to the backhand and the next time to the forehand. The problem is that your opponent will probably read the pattern.

I suggest you hit one or two serves straight at your opponent, hit one close to the center line, and then try a wide serve, followed by more serves straight at him again.

*Why is it that sometimes when we are ahead forty love on my serve we lose the game?*

You probably get careless. You relax. You think you're home free.

Frequently when a player is ahead forty love on his serve, he takes a wild chance and tries for an ace with his first serve and hits the second serve too hard and double-faults.

When I am ahead forty love on my serve, I play the next point in an orthodox or safe manner. If I lose the point, it's 40–15. At this time I might take a chance and go for the big serve. If I lose the point, I play the 40–30 point safely again. I never play all three points recklessly.

*What can I do if I must serve looking into the sun?*

When you serve on the sunny side of the court, look up to see where the sun is—don't look right into it—then adjust your toss so you don't put the ball right into the bright sunlight.

If the sun is directly over your head, for example, toss the ball a little to the right or a little farther forward than usual.

I have been in situations where the sun has been low enough for me to toss the ball through the sun and move my eyes up quickly through the bright spot to make contact with the ball above the sun.

## My Second Serve

*Do I serve from the same position?*

Yes, because your problem remains the same. You still want to be in the best position to cover your half of the court.

*Should my second serve be as hard as the first or should I just poop the ball in if that is the only way I can be certain of not double-faulting?*

If the only way you can get your second serve in is to poop it, then by all means do that because at least you get the ball in play. But if you must poop the second serve, then try to get it in as deep as possible. With a weak second serve, you should try that much harder to get a high percentage of your first serves in.

Try not to give the receiver a shallow second serve because he may drive it down your throat or your partner's.

One of the worst mistakes you can make in any doubles match is to double-fault. It's a cardinal sin, like walking the pitcher in baseball. Why *give* your opponents the point? If you get the ball in the court, at least your opponent has to beat you and perhaps he might make a mistake.

*Is there any way I can use a soft second serve to advantage?*

Not really, because a soft serve will probably put you and your partner on the defensive rather than the offensive. Sometimes even good players over-hit a soft serve, but they quickly get the proper range and then you will be in trouble.

*Should I follow a soft second serve to the net?*

That depends on your opponents. If they're any good at all, I don't recommend you follow a soft serve to the net because they'll probably kill you with the return.

If your second serve is consistently soft, your opponents will be standing well inside the baseline when receiving, which means they will be hitting the ball high in relationship to the net, allowing them to hit down at your feet more readily than if the ball was waist-high and they had to stand farther back.

*Is there any special type of serve a right-hander should hit to a left-handed receiver?*

When serving to the deuce court, you can try to slice the serve wide because a left-hander will have to stretch to get it with his backhand.

You might also try to serve tight to his forehand (toward his left hip) because the ball will follow him as he tries to step around to hit his forehand.

When serving to the ad court, you could serve straight at him, aiming at his left hip. Any balls that you serve up the center on the ad court will be coming in on his backhand.

*Does a left-handed server have an advantage over a right-handed receiver?*

Yes, because there are fewer left-handers playing the game, so a right-handed receiver is not as accustomed to the curve coming in the opposite way that it does when a right-hander serves to him. Conversely, a left-hander is not at a disadvantage when he sees a right-hander because he plays more right-handed players.

*What if I am unable to place the serve where I want?*

Get the serve in as deep as possible and make every effort to get the first serve in every time. Even if the first serve isn't deep, it will be more effective than a weak second serve.

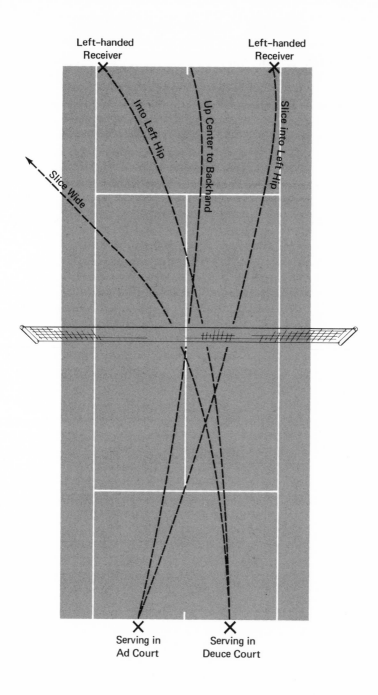

*I have seen some players serve underhand. Is that a legitimate serve and is it a good idea?*

It is legitimate but not recommended. Most players who serve underhand have a bad case of tennis elbow or some other injury. If they had a choice, they certainly wouldn't serve underhand.

You can, however, serve any way you wish— underhand, side-arm, or overhead. I don't recall anyone using an underhand serve that has ever played first-class tennis.

*What should I do if my opponent is constantly moving in on my second serve?*

If your second serve is weak, there really isn't any way for you to stop your opponent from moving in. If you get your first serve in more often, he won't be able to move in on your second serve.

When you get your first serve in he doesn't know what you're going to try. If you miss it, he knows your second serve is going to be weaker and probably a little more shallow.

*What can I do if my first serve is off?*

If your first serve is off, you should hit your second serve first. Get the ball in three or four times. Get the range and build up your confidence. Then you can start to pick up speed with your first serve if you want to.

Every airplane pilot has a takeoff and landing procedure or check list that must be followed. When I played championship tennis, I had a check list in my mind, so when I was not hitting a certain stroke as well as I wanted, I didn't get panicky; I just went down my check list. I discovered what I was doing wrong every time.

### TRABERT'S CHECK LIST FOR SERVING

A. Am I watching the ball until the moment of impact?
B. Am I holding the ball lightly between the first two fingertips and the thumb?
C. Am I tossing the ball up to the right of my body and forward of the baseline so that I am leaning into the serve when I hit it?
D. Am I tossing the ball to my maximum reach?
E. Is the head of my racket "scratching" my back?
F. Am I snapping my wrist at the ball?

## My Partner Serves

*Where should I stand when my partner is serving?*

Stand halfway between the service line and the net, facing the person who will return the ball. Be near enough to the alley so that you can take one stride and reach to cover it. You should also be able to take one stride and reach to cover the center of the court, which is your basic responsibility.

From this position—regardless of whether the

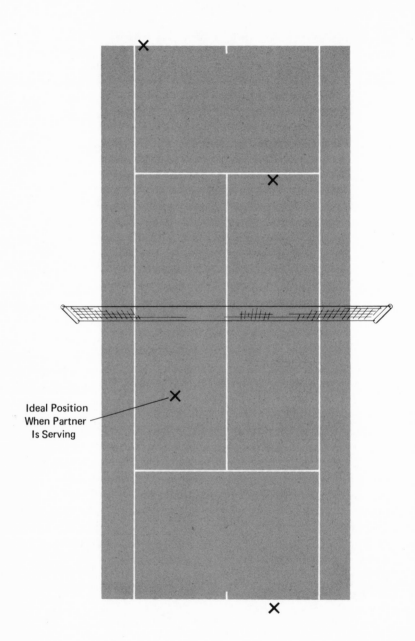

Ideal Position
When Partner
Is Serving

ball is returned high, low, hard, lobbed, or down your alley—you should have time to make your shot. You can move in if the ball comes high and softly, yet you will be less vulnerable to a lob. You have time to prepare if the ball is hit hard and/or low directly at you. And if the ball is intercepted by the opposing net man, you are in a position to help out.

*Do I keep the same position for both serves?*

Yes.

*Where is the best place for me to return the ball on the first volley?*

If you are volleying a ball that is well above the net, hit it down at the feet of the man closest to you at net. If you are volleying a ball that is low, hit to the man farthest from you or down the center. If your opponent stays back, volley as deep as possible.

*What should I do if my partner serves wide?*

Follow the receiver out wide to cut off a potential shot down your alley. Remember, the only ball your partner can't help you with is the one hit down your alley. Any cross-court return will be going toward your partner.

Even if you overplay and move too wide in the alley and your opponent hits a ball through your part of the middle court, it's still going toward your partner and he has a chance to get it. If you don't move out and cover your alley and the re- ceiver hits there, you've lost the point.

You can also maintain your position, inviting the receiver to go down the alley. If you do this, be aware that this is a likely possibility and pre- pare to cover the opening.

Or you can fake. Move your head and shoulders to make your opponent think you are going to poach. If you fake, however, be prepared for the ball to come down your alley and have your racket ready.

*Is there anything I can do if my partner's serves are always soft and easy to return?*

If there's such an imbalance in the players that your partner's soft serves enable your opponents to clobber you there's nothing you can do other than increase your life insurance.

*When I am playing net on my partner's serve to the ad court, should I poach on my backhand volley?*

As a rule I don't believe that poaching is a good idea. You should poach only occasionally and when you haven't moved for a while. Too often poaching is a hazard because you are not quick enough or skillful enough to judge the flight of the ball properly. You will either miss it or leave your original position too early, leaving time and a big opening for your opponent.

As for poaching on your backhand, that would depend on how good your backhand volley is. The average player is not capable of poaching effectively in that situation. Chances are the return of service that you poach on could be handled better by your partner because the ball is probably going to his forehand as he is coming into position after service. In all probability he can handle a forehand volley better than you can a backhand volley.

*Should I poach on my forehand volley when my partner is serving to the deuce court?*

If you poach you should be reasonably certain of your ability to put the ball away because you have left your side of the court unguarded. You probably are better with the forehand volley though.

*Is it better to poach off the first serve or the second?*

You should very rarely poach on a second serve because the receiver is standing closer, he has more time to make the shot, and you have less time to react. He might be able to run around a serve to his backhand and take it on his forehand, and if he knows you are in the habit of poaching, he will probably go down your alley.

*After I have poached, should I return to my original position at net?*

When you poach and physically cross the center service line, you should keep going so your

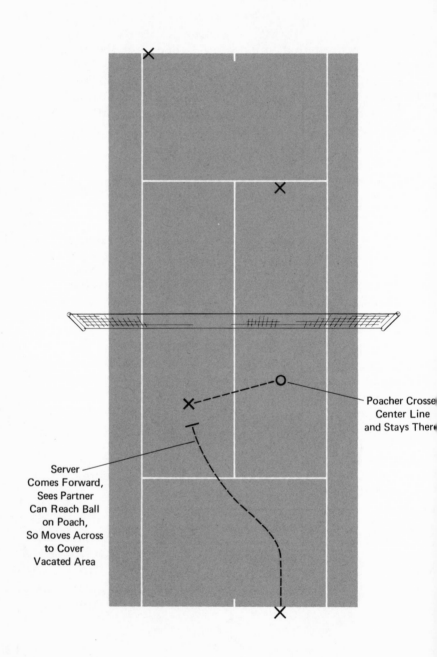

Poacher Crosses Center Line and Stays There

Server Comes Forward, Sees Partner Can Reach Ball on Poach, So Moves Across to Cover Vacated Area

partner automatically knows he should go the other way.

*What is the difference between poaching and "pigging"?*

Poaching is a timely sort of move made when you either want to disrupt your opponents or think you can make a point outright by taking a ball which your partner would normally handle.

Pigging is usually far less effective and disrupts your partner rather than your opponents.

Pigging is done only by selfish players or by people determined to win the match to the exclusion of his partner's pleasure. Even if you win the set by pigging all the balls, your partner will not have had a good time—so what was the point of playing?

You have to recognize why you're out on the court. For most players it's to have some fun, get some exercise, and to hit some balls, and a pigging partner spoils his partner's pleasure.

*My partner serves and stays back, and when the return of service comes to his backhand, he usually misses it. Is there anything I can do to help him?*

When he's serving to the deuce court, you might fake or actually move closer to the center line, trying to force the receiver to hit cross court to your partner's forehand.

When he's serving to the ad court, you might try playing Australian style. You stand just to the

## Australian Formation

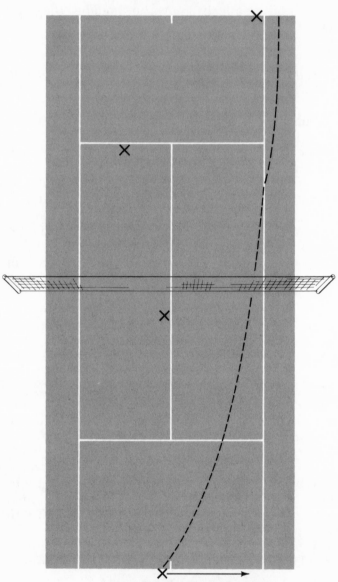

Server Moves to Right After Serving—
Return Will Come to Forehand

left of the center service line and your partner serves from the center of the baseline, preferably to the backhand of the receiver.

The Australian technique forces your opponents to hit directly to you at net or down the line to your partner's forehand, or attempt a lob over your head.

A word of caution, though. If you try the Australian technique, your partner must move instantly to his right after he serves in preparation for a return to his forehand.

*Where is the best place for me to stand?*

In the deuce court, stand with your feet on the baseline and your right foot on the singles sideline. If the serve does not have any spin on it, you can move a bit left toward the center of the court.

In the ad court, stand with your left foot about a foot or so from the singles sideline if the server is a right-hander. If a lefty is serving, your left foot should be on the singles sideline, maybe even farther over to your left, depending on his serve.

Most people should never be more than a few inches behind the baseline. The farther back you stand, the longer the ball has to make its maximum curve before reaching you. When possible, get to the ball before it has completed curving. Also the longer the ball travels to you and back, the more time the server has to get up to the net. The quicker you get the ball back, the less time the server has to get to his ideal position.

*What is the best stance for returning serve?*

Always face your problem. When returning service, your toes should be pointed toward the server. Your feet should be approximately shoulder-width apart. Weight should be forward on the balls of your feet with your knees bent and torso tilted slightly forward with your rear end tucked underneath so your weight is low.

A common error is for the receiver to stand with his toes parallel to the baseline rather than point-

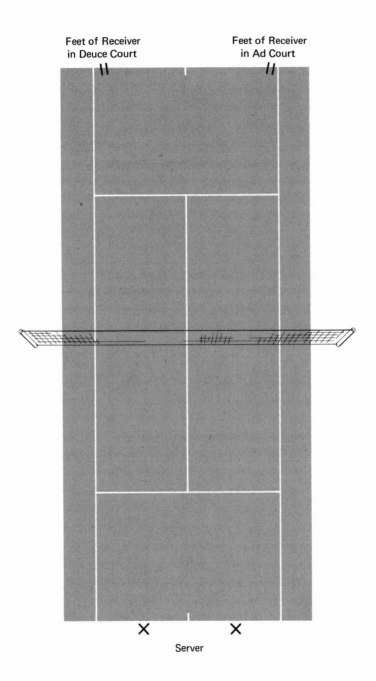

Feet of Receiver
in Deuce Court

Feet of Receiver
in Ad Court

×        ×

Server

ing at the server. In the ad court he has *less* distance to turn to hit his backhand return but in the deuce court he has *more* distance to turn to hit a backhand.

If you face the server, you have an equal distance to move or turn for either a forehand or a backhand return.

The racket should be held waist-high in front of you and parallel to the ground, pointing at the server.

*What grip should I have on my racket when awaiting service?*

It depends on the individual. If you are capable of making a grip-change quickly, it may be better to wait for the service with the racket prepared for your weaker return.

If the server consistently hits to your backhand, and it is your weaker stroke, you can hold the racket for a backhand return, and if the ball comes to the forehand you can make a quick adjustment.

Some players receive service with a grip midway between the backhand and forehand, when they are not certain where the serve is coming. That way they have only a small adjustment to make for either the forehand or backhand.

*Should I return a serve the same in doubles as in singles?*

Your problems are obviously different because in doubles you are basically restricted to a cross-court return. The premise of hitting the ball low in relationship to your opponent's body as he comes to the net is the same, however. And if he stays back, *depth* is the byword.

You don't return the same way, which is one reason why good singles players are not always good doubles players. Mechanically they may not be able to hit the ball with control and get it low over the top of the net, falling short in the court as the player is coming in or when he's at the net.

*How can I handle a hard serve to my backhand?*

As soon as the ball is tossed in the air by the server and you know it is coming to your backhand you should:

Watch the ball carefully.

Simultaneously use your free hand to turn the racket to your backhand grip and help pull the racket back alongside your body in the proper backhand hitting position.

Grip the racket tightly and keep a firm wrist.

When the ball bounces you should:

Lean into it and don't let it push you backward.

You may find that a shorter backswing will help too.

Follow through.

*Is it safe to run around my backhand on the first serve?*

Not unless the serve is hit slowly. If the serve has any kind of speed, you probably won't be able to run around it successfully.

*What can I do if the serve is consistently to my
weak backhand?*

Move one step further toward the center line
in the deuce court and prepare yourself with a
backhand grip. In the ad court you can move one
step to your left. Don't take a big backswing but
don't forget a full follow-through. Keep your wrist
firm.

*How can I handle a serve to my forehand that
is very fast and hard for me to return?*

Your problem is probably not getting the racket
ready in time. Take a shorter backswing with
a normal follow-through and keep the wrist very
firm. The combination of a shorter swing, the
firmness of your contact with the ball, and its
speed will help give you a good return of service.
Don't straighten up as you hit.

*What can I do if the net man poaches on my
service returns?*

Try to hit the ball down his alley more often.
This is a difficult and risky shot, however.

It's often a good idea to hit the ball straight at
the net man because he has the added complica-
tion of trying to get his body out of the way.

If he poaches some and also fakes some
poaches, you might trap him if you hit the ball
right at him.

If he's a good poacher and faker, hit just past
his right hip in the deuce court and just past

his left hip in the ad court, because if a person is faking he fakes toward the middle and comes back to cover the ball that he's inviting you to hit down the alley. If it's not a fake and he continues to move, he's gone beyond the point where he was originally, so your shot will be good.

Your best tactic is a good cross-court return, and in this instance I would say to myself, "I'm not going to pay any attention to the net man. I'm going to concentrate on watching the ball, knowing that if I do hit a good cross-court shot, he can't get to it."

You can occasionally try to punch a lob over the net man's head. A decent offensive lob might be difficult for him to handle, particularly if it's made over his backhand side because most poachers move close to the net.

*How can I improve the angle of my return of service?*

Good players seldom try for sharply angled returns of service. It's a hard shot to make consistently, so my advice is to forget it.

A good cross-court shot is fine, but a sharp angle is a dangerous shot. It's too easy to miss for the number that you're going to make successfully. It's what I call a low-percentage shot.

*How can I learn the angled dink return the touring pros use?*

That's too tough a shot for the average player to attempt. If you try it and don't hit the ball perfectly, it will sit up in the air where your opponent can move in and put it away. Or you may hit the ball past the sideline or into the net.

If you are capable of hitting a dink or soft ball with control, try to hit down the middle of the court, because that kind of return does not open up your court. Your opponents have less angle on the attempted return.

Even if the dink return isn't hit perfectly you have a better chance of staying out of trouble if you hit down the middle.

*Is there any way I can hit the ball closer to the top of the net to keep my opponents from getting too many put aways on my return of service?*

Lower your sights. If you shoot a gun at a target and the bullet hits high, you don't change the speed of the bullet, you lower your sights.

You are probably swinging at the ball on an upward plane, so flatten the swing a little.

*What should I do if the server stands wide?*

Follow the server out, because that means it's going to be difficult for him to hit a serve down the middle where you can't reach it. In effect, the nearer the server stands toward the center, the nearer you move toward the center. The wider he stands, the wider you stand.

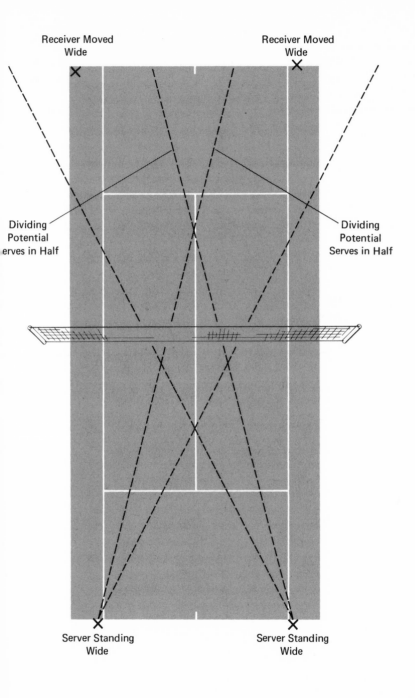

Receiver Moved
Wide

Receiver Moved
Wide

Dividing
Potential
erves in Half

Dividing
Potential
Serves in Half

Server Standing
Wide

Server Standing
Wide

*I play the ad court against two opponents who are lefties. The service comes wide to my back-and and the lefty at the net is capable of reaching midcourt with his forehand. I don't have enough control to make the angled cross-court return. Is there anything I can do?*

You are probably not standing far enough to your left when you are waiting for the serve, which means a wide serve is running you out of the court and you are hitting late.

More farther to your left so you have a good cross-court shot that is going away from the net man.

If the serve is wide and the net man goes wide with you, he leaves you all the more space to make a cross-court return.

If the service is wide and the net man has a tendency to inch toward the center, you have to keep the net man honest by hitting down his alley a few times.

*Is there anything typical about a left-hander's serve?*

Yes, the curve. A left-handed server's balls curve from your right to your left. A good lefty generally serves to the backhand of a right-handed receiver, which gives him an advantage because most right-handed tennis players are accustomed to right-handed servers and balls which curve from their left to their right.

If a right-hander serves toward your right hip and you are right-handed, the ball curves to your forehand, allowing for a smooth forehand re-

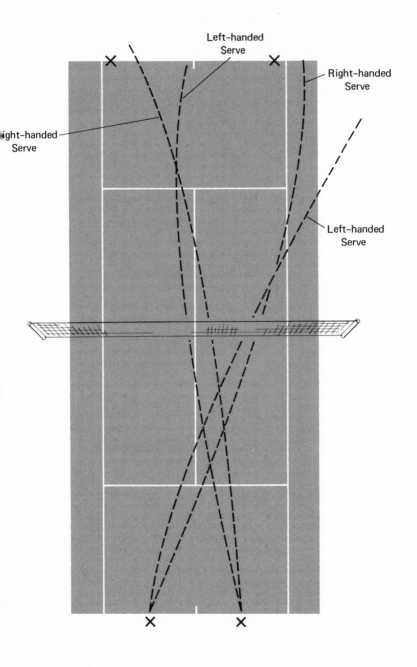

turn. But a left-handed serve to your right hip curves into your body the opposite way.

Most left-handers serving to the deuce court will go down the centerline to a right-hander's backhand, and when the ball bounces, it will run away from the receiver.

When a left-handed server hits tight to your forehand, you're better off letting the ball go to the left of your body and returning it with your backhand. If he serves to your backhand, be prepared to reach out for the ball which will swing away from you, just like a right-hander's slice runs away from a righty on the forehand side.

*How can I prepare to receive a left-hander's serve?*

When he is serving to the deuce court, you should (if you are right-handed) stand a little more toward the center and anticipate a probable backhand return.

When he's serving to the ad court, you can stand with your left foot on the singles sideline. If his serve has a big curve, you might even straddle the singles sideline.

*Tip:* WHENEVER A LEFTY SERVES TO YOU, A RIGHT-HANDER, YOU MIGHT PREPARE YOUR RACKET FOR A BACKHAND RETURN.

*Is there anything I can do to upset the server's rhythm and concentration?*

It's legitimate for you to stand in different positions from your normal one. If a man is hitting big serves, try standing four or five feet behind the baseline. His instinct might be to hit a soft spin and rush the net quickly. As soon as he throws the ball up in the air to serve, move quickly to your normal position. If this doesn't work, you haven't lost anything because he has been hurting you with his serve anyway.

You can also stand further to the left or the right, but be prepared to cover the opening you've created. All you're doing in this instance is giving the server something additional to think about.

Remember, however, if you stand outside of your original or normal position for receiving service, you should stand still until the server has thrown the ball up in the air. You must not be moving around while the server is looking at you. But once the ball is tossed up in the air for the serve, you're entitled to move any place you wish.

*What is my best percentage shot for a service return?*

You should hit the return of service cross court over the center of the net where it's lower (36 inches) than any other place (42 inches over the doubles sideline).

Hit to the man nearest to you at net only when you think you can win the point outright.

*When the server rushes the net what is my best return?*

Return as low as possible. A good return is not based on speed; it's based on direction. If you hit the ball a little more softly so it drops at the

Return Serve
Cross Court
Basically Over
Center of Net

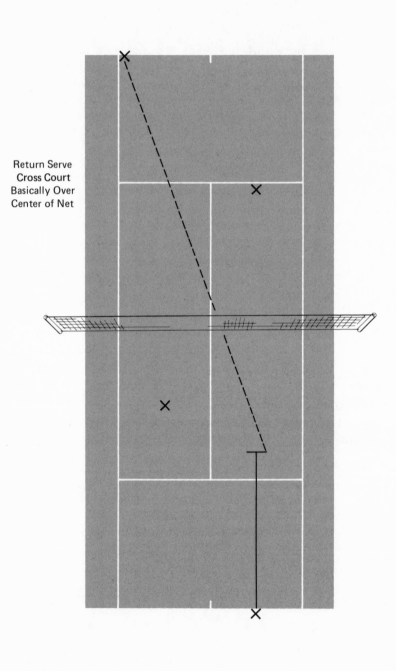

opponent's feet, that's generally a far more effective return than hitting it twice as hard but at his waist level where he can volley it more easily.

*What is the best way to handle:*

*A slice serve.* You can usually tell a serve is going to be sliced because the toss is to the right of the server's body.

A slice serve turns in the air just like a curved pitch in baseball, so you have to judge the amount of bend the ball will make because it's not coming in a straight line.

When a right-hander serves a slice to another right-hander, the ball will either curve away from him on the forehand side or curve into him on the backhand.

In the deuce court it is usually better to take the serve on your forehand whenever possible, because when you've completed your shot, you will be in the center of your part of the court in a good position.

In the ad court, if you take the serve on your backhand, you will be nearer the center of the court after your shot. However, the slice comes into your body on the backhand.

*Rule of thumb:* ON A SLICE SERVE, TAKE IT ON YOUR FOREHAND WHENEVER POSSIBLE.

*Top-spin or American Twist serve:* You can tell when this serve is coming. The toss is over the server's left shoulder, because this is the only way he can make the ball jump to the side.

The serve normally loops over the net and bounces high, kicking off to your left.

Since this is one of the most difficult serves for the average player to return, you must prepare properly for it.

Since the ball is going to kick or bounce higher than normal, prepare your racket at the height where you are going to make contact with the ball.

If the serve is to your backhand, you can try to block it by taking a very short jabbing stroke like a high backhand volley.

If the serve is to your forehand, prepare the racket high and swing through the ball. Be careful not to swing down at the ball or you'll probably hit it into the net.

Personally, I hit over the ball, using top spin, because that helps bring the ball back down in the court.

*Tip:* STEP IN AND TAKE A TWIST OR TOP-SPIN SERVE AS EARLY AS POSSIBLE BECAUSE THAT WILL GIVE THE BALL LESS CHANCE TO JUMP OFF TO THE SIDE. YOU'D BETTER WATCH IT CLOSELY, THOUGH!

*Flat serve.* This serve comes on you very quickly and the ball usually bounces about waist level.

*Tip:* SHORTEN YOUR BACKSWING AND USE A NORMAL FOLLOW-THROUGH WITH A FIRM WRIST, USING THE SPEED OF THE BALL TO YOUR ADVANTAGE. STAY LOW—DON'T STRAIGHTEN UP.

*Is there any way I can determine what kind of serve is going to be hit to me?*

You should be watching the server's toss carefully. Not only must you watch the ball as part of your concentration but you can tell from the toss what kind of serve is *not* going to be hit.

For example, if the ball is thrown to the right of the server's body, there is no way he can hit an American Twist serve. The best thing he can do with that toss is hit a flat or sliced serve.

If the ball is thrown to the left of his body, there is no way he can slice the ball effectively. He will be hitting a kick serve.

*How should I "read" the toss?*

You should generally move a little in the opposite direction from the toss. If the ball is tossed to the server's right, he is usually going to hit to your right. If the toss is to the left, the serve will probably go to your left.

## Second Serve

*Should I keep the same position for the second serve?*

When your opponent has missed his first serve, take a step forward. He is not likely to serve the second as hard or as deep, and if he does, he is not going to get many in. There is a corollary between his missing the first serve and what you can do to take advantage of it.

Some players make the mistake of moving too far in on the second serve, however. It is always better to have to go forward rather than backward for the ball. Whenever possible you want your weight advancing when you make contact with the ball.

*Is it all right to run around a serve hit to my backhand?*

If you know that a second service is going to be slow and your forehand is stronger than your backhand, you should run around the ball as soon as it leaves the server's racket and return the ball as deep as possible unless your opponent rushes to the net. If he does that, try to hit down at his feet.

*Where is the best place to return a second serve?*

You should rarely hit the ball at the net man if there's somebody in the backcourt unless you are close to the net man and can hit down at him. The net man is always a threat, because even if he misplays a ball he might do something with it while the man in the backcourt can't hurt you as easily.

*Rule of thumb:* NEVER HIT THE BALL AT THE NET MAN IF THERE'S A MAN ON THE BASELINE UNLESS YOU THINK YOU CAN WIN THE POINT OUT-RIGHT WITH THAT ONE SHOT.

Seldom hit back down the line because you're asking for trouble. If you misjudge or mistime the shot, you will probably hit wide because you are shooting at a small area. It's better to aim into the center of the court or hit straight back at the man furthest from you.

Forget about angling your shots. They are too risky and if you are in a position to angle the ball, you're also in a position to hit a good solid shot that will probably win for you. If it doesn't, you are still in a better situation than if you've hit wide. It opens up your entire court.

*What is the best way to handle a dink or soft second serve?*

This should be the simplest serve of all to handle but many people get so anxious to kill the ball that they take their eyes off it or forget their mechanics, especially early racket preparation.

One way to handle a soft serve is to shorten your backswing and concentrate on watching the ball until the point of contact. Step in close because the ball is not coming fast. Catch it fairly high on the bounce so you hit down at your opponent's feet if he is coming to the net. If he is staying back, go for depth and come to the net behind your return.

If you still aren't successfully hitting the soft serve, it's probably because you think it's too easy and you are still taking your eyes off the ball.

*What can I do if someone is serving before I am ready?*

The rule is that if someone has served before you are ready and you make no obvious attempt to return the ball but just hold up your hand and say, "I'm sorry, I wasn't ready," they must serve the point over. But if you try for the ball and miss it, you've lost the point.

If you're settling into position and you see the server starting before you're ready, hold up your hand to stop him. I've done that at Wimbledon on several occasions.

You can also get into position keeping your head down and looking at your feet until you're ready. He can't start serving until you look up.

### CHECK LIST FOR SERVICE RETURN

A. Am I watching the ball?
B. Am I getting the racket back quickly enough?
C. Am I taking too big a swing at the ball?
D. Am I straightening up as I contact the ball?
E. Am I standing in the best possible place on the court?
F. Am I keeping my wrist locked in a firm position?

## My Partner Receives

*Where should I stand?*

You should stand with your heels just inside the service line midway between the center service line and the singles sideline. That way if the man at net intercepts the service return and volleys it back through the center, you have a chance to reach the ball. If your partner hits a good low return, move forward because the ball will be rising up over the net toward one of you and you may be able to volley it down.

*Should I watch my partner as he receives the ball?*

Many players make that mistake and are unable to react quickly to the type of shot their partner has hit.

I suggest you watch the net man's eyes. His reaction will tell you what your partner has done with the ball. If his eyes get big as saucers, you know the ball is going to him. If he stands still without reaction, you know the ball is going to his partner, so you switch back to him.

Your number-one threat is always the man closest to you, so try to watch him whenever possible.

*When should I move forward from this starting position?*

Hold your position at the service line until your partner has made a good return and it has cleared the man at the net. If his return is low, move forward. If it is high, hold your position.

*Is there any time when my partner is receiving when I ought to be in the backcourt with him?*

You might try playing the backcourt with your partner if the opposing net man is poaching suc-

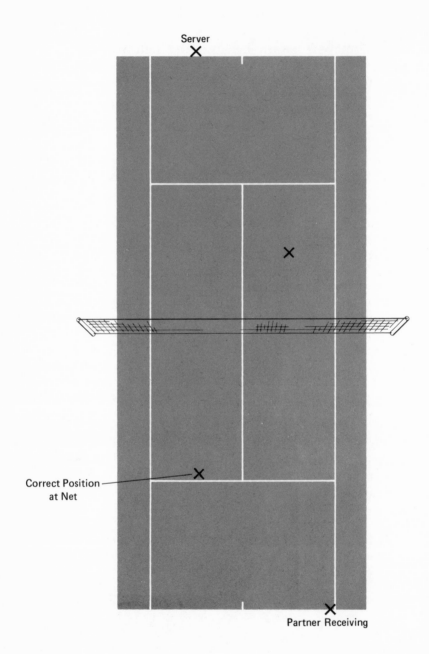

Server

X

Correct Position
at Net

Partner Receiving

cessfully. By staying in the backcourt you have time to go for the balls which the net man has been putting away. But you must always be ready to move up to the net at the first opportunity.

*How can I help out if the server is constantly hitting serves to my partner's weak backhand?*

There is not much you can do.

You can stand closer to the center service line when your partner is receiving. Sometimes this can influence the server into hitting wider in the court. But you must get into your position before the server starts to serve.

*When we are down forty love on our opponents' serve, should we go for a winner or play it safe?*

If you're not tired, play the point regularly and try to win it. If you're a service-break down you should do everything except run through the fence to get the point because you need the service-break.

# 5.
# HOW TO
# VOLLEY

*What is a volley?*

A volley is a ball that you hit before it bounces either on the right or left side of your body.

*Where should I stand?*

Remember the premise of doubles: You are trying to cut your opponent's possibilities in half and divide your responsibility with your partner.

Your best position is midway between the net and the service line and about midway between the center service line and the singles sideline.

You don't want to be so far away from the net that it's easy for your opponents to get balls down at your feet and you don't want to be in so close that it's easy for them to get a lob over your head.

If you stand where I suggest, you will have more time to react to a fast return and it will be very difficult for your opponents to hit an offensive lob over your head. With a step and reach in either direction, you should be able to cover the alley and your obligation in the center.

*What is the proper stance?*

Always crouch down while at the net and straighten up only when you must reach for a high ball. Your knees should be bent and your rear end tucked under with your weight slightly

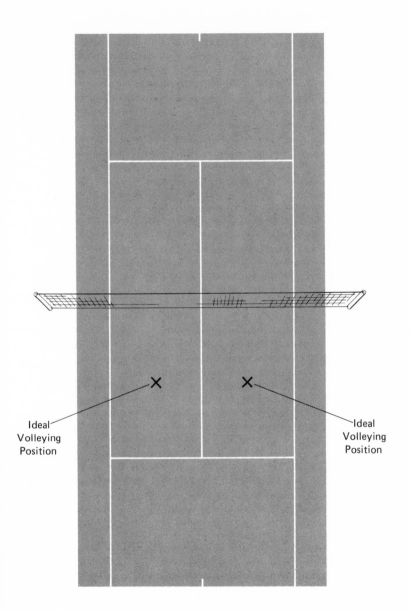

Ideal
Volleying
Position

Ideal
Volleying
Position

forward on the balls of your feet. Bend slightly forward at the waist, and your feet should be spread shoulder width. Never stand flat-footed or anchored in one spot. Be like a boxer who is always in motion. If your feet are moving, you will be surprised at how much quicker you can react.

When you are volleying, you must bend at the knees and waist so your eyes are on a level with the flight of the ball. This is true of any stroke but especially true when you are volleying, because if you are standing erect you may not think the ball is coming over the net. If you are bent down, you can judge the flight of the ball and its height. Like shooting a gun—it is more accurate sighting down the barrel than shooting from the hip.

When you are standing up straight, your weight is on your heels but as soon as you bend your knees and your torso forward, the weight automatically transfers to your toes, which makes you quicker. You're in the ready position, enabling you to move quickly in any direction.

Also, when you are volleying at net and your knees are bent and an opponent tries to hit a lob over your head, you're in a position to jump because your knees are already bent. If you were standing with your knees straight, you would have to dip and try to jump and by that time the ball might be over your head.

Your eyes should be down as near as possible to the flight of the ball with the racket head kept above the net at chin level, because most balls will come to you fairly high.

If a ball comes at you shoulder height, you are in good shape because your eyes are on a level with the ball. If the ball comes to you low over the net, don't make the common error of just dropping the racket head down. Instead, get the racket low, more or less parallel to the ground, by bending down as on a low forehand or backhand.

Many players who take the ready position at net make the mistake of having their elbows alongside and touching their body. I suggest you extend your arms forward comfortably so your elbows are a few inches ahead of your body. Your free hand should be on the throat of the racket, ready to help pull it back to get it ready. If your arms are extended forward and you lay the racket head back for a forehand volley, you can see the ball and make contact well in front of your body.

Oscillate your upper body and the racket while watching the ball in play but don't turn your feet and twist all around to follow the action. Just turn your torso.

*A tip:* UNDER PRESSURE, STAY LOW RATHER THAN STRAIGHTEN UP.

## *How should I hold my racket?*

If you're going to hold just one grip on your racket it should be between the forehand and backhand grip, not extreme on one side or the other.

If you hold an extreme forehand grip, for example, it may mean that your backhand volley will be quite weak. If you hold an absolute backhand grip, your forehand volley may be weak.

But if you hold a grip that's midway between the two, you have a chance to hit fairly well on either side.

*A suggestion:* IF YOU'RE IN THE DEUCE COURT AT THE NET, MOST BALLS ARE GOING TO COME TO YOUR RIGHT, SOMEWHERE THROUGH THE CENTER, SO YOU MIGHT CHEAT A LITTLE TOWARD THE FOREHAND GRIP BECAUSE, AGAIN, MOST BALLS WILL BE GOING THROUGH THE CENTER.

In short, I suggest you hold the grip that is going to be strongest for your handling balls down the center. This will take some experimenting on your part before you are able to decide which grip is best for you.

*How should I position the racket?*

The racket head should be above your hand pointed slightly upward and higher than the top of the net. The arm holding the racket should be comfortably extended forward so the elbow is forward of your body.

## Forehand Volley

The *forehand volley* is the only stroke in which your wrist is not in a natural position at impact. The hand should be laid back so the palm is parallel to the net.

Have a friend toss a ball to you at shoulder-height on your right side. Catch the ball and hold it in the position in which it was caught. Look at your hand. You'll see that it is laid back. There's no other way you can catch a ball with your right hand.

When making a forehand volley, turn sideways to the ball when possible and lay your hand back as though you were catching the ball. You want the racket head to be coming at the ball from slightly above with the racket face laid open, the head of the racket a little above your hand.

Hit from behind the ball with a forward chopping motion because you want to impart some back spin.

The racket head should not move ahead of your wrist. The hand, laid back, remains firm in the locked position and there should be little backswing or follow-through. Just punch the ball, using the elbow for movement to help make the stroke.

*How can I aim a forehand volley?*

To hit cross court, catch the ball a little earlier. To hit down the line, catch the ball a little farther back. In either case, make contact in front of your body.

*What should I do with my free hand?*

The free hand helps you change grips and prepare the racket. It should be on the throat of the racket at all times between shots.

*Is it better to hit down the center of the court softly or with power?*

If the ball comes to you above the top of the net, you should hit down with power. If the ball is below the top of the net, you can't hit hard and keep it in play so take some speed off and try to go for depth if there is a man on the baseline. If both opponents are at net, try to hit the ball softly so it drops at their feet.

The sign of a good volley at net is not always speed but frequently finesse. Watch the best doubles players in the world clustered at the net, and they sometimes play a cat and mouse game, hitting the ball softly and keeping it low over the net. No one dares hit the ball hard because a rising ball can be hit back down at them. Whenever possible the ball should be kept below the opponent's waist level.

*Rule of thumb:* WHEN THE BALL COMES TO YOU WELL ABOVE THE NET, YOU SHOULD TRY TO DO SOMETHING AGGRESSIVE WITH IT. WHEN IT'S BELOW THE NET, THINK OF STAYING OUT OF TROUBLE.

*Why is it that when I am coming to my volleying position at the net I am frequently caught unprepared for the volley?*

Chances are you are making the same mistake you make when rushing the net after serving. Never take a volley on the run. When your opponent is about to make his shot, you should stop, straddle, and make the volley. Then go forward again to the desired position.

*Why are so many of my low volleys going into the net?*

There are several possibilities.

You may not be laying the racket face open to make the ball rise back over the net.

You may not be bending down low enough, which means you are probably misjudging the flight of the ball.

You may be taking your eyes off the ball because you want to see where you are going to hit it and where your opponents have moved.

Or you may be trying to hit the ball too hard.

When the ball is down below the top of the net, my only thought is to stay out of trouble. If one of my opponents is at the baseline, I try to volley deep toward him. My deep volley pushes him back four or five feet behind the baseline which keeps me out of trouble.

If my opponents are at net and I have a low volley, I try to drop the ball back over the net softly so that it is at their feet, forcing them to hit the ball up so I can volley it down.

*How can I hit a volley so that it just drops over the net?*

That's called a drop volley and it is used when your opponents are in the backcourt and you are at the net.

Hold your racket out as though you were going to make a regular volley but as you make contact with the ball, pull the racket back slightly, taking some speed off the ball, instead of punching forward in the direction of your opponent. You are, in effect, cushioning the ball with your racket. How far you pull the racket back depends on how fast the ball is traveling and how near you are to the net.

## Backhand Volley

The *backhand volley* is made when you are at net and the ball comes to your left.

The mechanics are the same as those for the forehand volley except that you don't lay the wrist back and you use your backhand grip whenever possible.

Turn sideways to the net when time permits and punch at the ball, using a short backswing and short follow-through. The racket face should be tilted slightly open to give back spin for control.

*What should I do with my free hand?*

It should be on the throat of your racket until you start the racket forward on the volley.

When making backhand volleys, I suggest you use your free hand to give the racket a little push forward.

## Half Volley

The *half volley* is made when the ball has been hit alongside or directly in front of your feet. You hit it just after it hits the ground.

Bend your knees so you're not just dropping the head of the racket and try to keep the racket approximately parallel to the ground. Get your head down so you are really watching the ball and

66

take a very short backswing and stroke the ball up from the ground with little follow-through.

You never want to swing from above the ball when making a half volley. If you do, you'll be hitting down on the ball. Just get the racket low and parallel to the ground, giving you the maximum amount of racket face for contact and come through the ball on a slightly upward plane.

*Where should I try to hit a half volley?*

When returning a half volley, your only thought should be to stay out of trouble. If your opponents are on the baseline, try to float the ball deep. If your opponents are at net, try to hit it low and softly in the hope that they will have to hit up to you.

# Lob Volley

The *lob volley* is one of the most delicate strokes in tennis and is seldom successfully used even by professionals.

You will see it used occasionally when all four players are at net and one of them attempts to pop a short lob over the head of his opponent. The problem is that if you hit a lob volley too short, your opponent will straighten up and knock it down your throat. If you hit it a little too hard, the ball will go past the baseline. I don't recommend you try it very often.

The flight of a tennis ball is dictated by how

much you lay the face of the racket open. For a lob volley you lay the face of the racket open and give the ball a short punch. The elevation of the racket face makes the ball to go up into the air quickly.

### CHECK LIST FOR THE VOLLEY

A.  Am I watching the ball?
B.  Am I keeping the wrist locked or firm and in one position?
C.  Am I punching at the ball?
D.  Am I making contact well in front of my body?
E.  Am I keeping the racket face slightly open?
F.  Am I coming down from above the ball?
G.  Am I standing up too straight?
H.  Am I turning sideways to the net when time permits?

## Overhead Smash

The *overhead smash* is made when a ball is hit over your head at net in the air or when you must run back to or behind the baseline to smash a high bouncing lob.

The safest way to make good contact with an overhead smash is to hit the ball with the face of the racket flat like a flat serve.

Your racket should be flat behind the ball as though you were going to hit your palm against a wall. That way you'll get the most speed and you'll make good contact even if you're off the center of the racket a bit.

A few suggestions:

Prepare the racket early by getting it behind you as though you are going to scratch your back with it. If you do this, your wrist will automatically be cocked.

Always snap your wrist when you hit an overhead smash just as you do when serving.

If you have to retreat to hit an overhead, turn sideways and shuffle back, bringing your feet together without crossing them. That way you will never have your weight falling back when you swing. If you're not certain just how far to retreat, remember it's better to retreat too far back and then come forward into the ball rather than not retreating far enough and then have your weight falling back as you hit.

Never hit an overhead softly. If you can get your racket on the ball, you can give it a ride.

Whenever possible try to hit an overhead on the right side of your body as when serving (on the left side if you are a lefty). Don't get the ball lined up over your head or on the left side.

Aim an overhead smash down the center of the court. Angles are risky and a smash is difficult enough to control without trying for angles. Don't hit too near the sidelines because you may mistime the ball and hit it out.

*Why is it that although I try to hit my overhead smashes the same as I would a serve I invariably mistime the ball?*

You're probably taking too much of a backswing, preparing the racket too late, or not watching the ball till impact.

Take a shorter backswing. Remember that when you are hitting an overhead the ball is falling rapidly so you must watch the ball very carefully.

*How can I avoid hitting overhead smashes into the net?*

Chances are you are making one of several common errors.

You may be taking your eyes off the ball before you make contact. An overhead smash is like a serve and you must try to see the racket make contact with the ball.

It's also possible that you are letting the ball drop too low before you make contact with it. Again, as in serving, you must lean into the ball to hit an overhead, stretching to your maximum reach when you make contact. This gives you a better angle into the court.

You could be positioned too far behind the ball, in which case your racket is coming straight down when you make contact. This is a common error people also make when serving: They toss the ball so far forward that they hit it down into the net.

### CHECK LIST FOR THE OVERHEAD SMASH

A. Are you watching the ball?
B. Are you hitting the ball in front of you and to the right of your body?
C. Are you snapping the wrist?
D. Did you prepare the racket early enough?
E. Did you position yourself far enough behind the ball so that you stepped or leaned into it?
F. Did you take too big a backswing?

# 6.
# HOW TO
# PLAY NET

*What is my obligation at the net?*

To divide your opponent's possibilities in half and your responsibility in half with your partner.

If you are in the proper position, you can step and reach in either direction and cover the alley or the center of the court. If your partner covers his alley plus his responsibility in the center, both of you will have your entire side of the court protected.

*What is the purpose of playing net?*

The main reason for going to the net is to force your opponent to try to hit a good shot. He must hit the ball fairly close to the top of the net, because if he hits it high you can volley it down at his feet or put it away. In trying to hit a good shot, the chances are he will either hit the ball out or put it where you can reach it.

While you are at the net, you are in an offensive position, putting constant pressure on your opponents because they are obliged to make good shots.

In championship doubles, the majority of points are won at the net!

*Who takes which ball?*

*Rule of thumb:* IF A BALL GOES DOWN THE CENTER OF THE COURT BETWEEN YOU AND YOUR PART-

NER, THE MAN CROSS COURT FROM THE OPPONENT
THAT HITS THE BALL TAKES IT BECAUSE IT'S COM-
ING TOWARD HIM AND GOING AWAY FROM HIS
PARTNER.

Sometimes situations arise when one partner is
closer to the net and a floating ball comes over the
net. If the man in front wants to take the shot, he
should make the commitment because the man
in back can see what he's doing. The man in back
should "clear out" to give his partner an unre-
stricted shot at the ball.

If both partners are at the net and a ball is coming at a reachable height down the center, the man
in the ad court should usually take it because it's
on his overhead or right side. If there's any doubt,
the man who has the ball on his serving side
should take the overhead.

*Which opponent should I concentrate on?*

While your partner is serving, you should concentrate on the man who is receiving the serve.
Once the ball is in play, watch the man closest
to you when possible and, if he doesn't react when
your partner has hit his shot, shift your attention
to the other opponent.

*Where should I try to place the ball?*

Your most effective shot is usually low and
down the center of the court because it lessens
the opponents' angle of return. The fact that it is
low means neither opponent can hit the ball hard

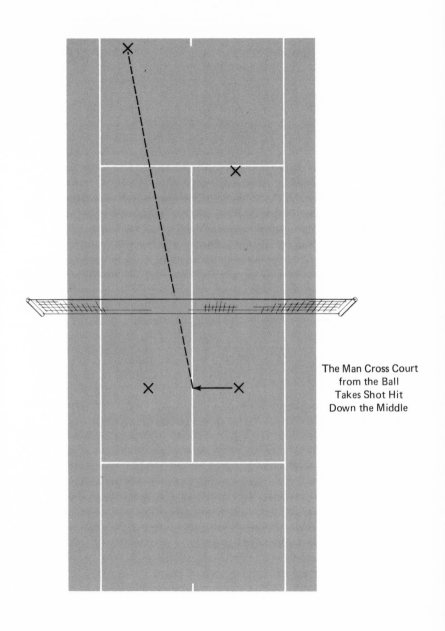

The Man Cross Court
from the Ball
Takes Shot Hit
Down the Middle

and keep it in court. In any event, one of them has to lift a low ball up at you, which means you can volley it back down at them.

If one of your opponents is at the net and the other is in the backcourt, you should try for depth, hitting to the man at the baseline because the ball must travel all that distance to get to him and must come all the way back, thus giving you time to get into a good position.

*Rule of thumb:* WHENEVER ONE OF YOUR OPPONENTS IS IN THE BACKCOURT, HIT TO HIM AND STAY AWAY FROM THE NET MAN UNLESS YOU CAN WIN THE POINT WITH THAT ONE SHOT DIRECTED AT THE NET MAN.

If you're in a good offensive position and the ball comes to you high over the net, then hit it down at the feet of the man closest to you. Chances of his scooping the ball up and putting it where you can't reach it for another shot are slim. There's no way an aggressive return can be made if a man has to pick the ball up at his feet. Another good place to hit the ball at an opponent playing net is directly at his right hip because the racket in his hand is angled across to the left side of his body. He can hit anything to his left or right if he reacts quickly enough. But if the ball comes directly at his right hip, he can't get the racket head in position quickly enough to make a return. By getting the ball in at his right hip, you've compounded his problems because he has the added problem of getting his body out of the way to make the return.

*Should I try to hit for angled returns?*

Forget about sharply angled or cute shots. They will get you in trouble more often than not because an angled shot opens up your court.

If you're in a position to angle a shot, chances are you can also hit the ball through the center or punch it at the feet or right hip of the opponent nearest to you.

*Why is it that I sometimes get trapped in quick exchanges at the net?*

Most players get trapped because they are standing up straight with the weight on their heels. They are anchored in position.

Or they take too big a swing at the volley. Before they can stop the follow-through, the ball has come right back to them before they have time to prepare. Always bring the racket back to the ready position after you have completed any stroke, including the volley.

Another reason some players get trapped is that they stand at the net with the racket head parallel to the ground and below the top of the net or at the same height. The ball will not often come at that level. Since it usually comes higher, it's better to have the racket at the anticipated height.

*Rule of thumb:* AFTER MAKING A VOLLEY AT THE NET, RETURN THE RACKET TO THE READY POSITION. THIS GOES FOR ANY OTHER STROKE YOU MAKE.

It will also help if you remember to use your free hand to help get the racket into the hitting position.

*What can I do with a partner who plays the backcourt well but is a dead loss at the net?*

Leave him in the backcourt while you play net and try to poach occasionally, or fake in hopes of influencing your opponents to hit down your alley.

*When do we retreat from the net?*

The only time you should give up possession of the net is when your opponents have hit an offensive lob which you or your partner must run back to get. Then both of you should retreat a few feet behind the baseline because the only safe return is a defensive lob which your opponents will probably smash back. As soon as a short ball is hit into your court, you should both get back to the net after you return their shot.

*Must I guard my alley when I am at net?*

You should be conscious of protecting your alley but too many people playing net have a tendency to hug the sidelines. This gives your opponents the feeling that they have all the room in the world and allows them to be relaxed when hitting. It also gives them more court in which to hit.

Even while protecting your alley you can make head and shoulder fakes to remind your opponents that you are always a threat to poach.

*What should I do if a shot is hit cross court wide of my alley?*

If the man in front of you doesn't follow you out, then you have a clear shot down his alley. If he moves out, then hit the ball low and over the center of the net.

Many people make the mistake of trying to out-angle the angler. They ask for trouble if they don't hit the ball perfectly.

Hit the ball low over the net and down the center and you will probably stay out of trouble. If one opponent stays back, then hit at him with depth.

*What is the best way to handle a heavy top-spin lob at the net?*

When a player hits a heavily topped lob it travels more quickly over your head and then drops down fast. Many players mistime the speed of the ball as it is dropping and hit it low on the racket near the throat.

When I see a heavily topped ball coming at me, I punch it like a high volley because I know it's difficult to handle. It's safer to volley the return even though you are reaching over your head.

*Why is it that when there is no pressure on me and I get into a position where I can make the point, I frequently miss an easy shot?*

After you've moved your opponent around and set up the ball so you can make the point, there's no excuse for not trying to put it away. If you don't, all the work you've done to get to that spot has been wasted.

Some players are tentative when they go for an easy or high ball because they think that it's a sin to miss that shot. Don't play it safe. If you get that ball up above the top of the net, do something aggresssive with it. Go for the knockout punch. You may miss some of the easy shots but the attempt must still be aggressive and you must try to put easy shots away. In the long run you'll be more effective. Don't forget to keep your eyes on the ball. Don't get careless.

*When we are playing at the net, is it better for my partner and me to be nearer to the center service line or to the alleys?*

If the ball is in the center of your opponent's court, you can both shift a little more toward the center of your own court. If the ball is wide, then the man in front of the wide player should move wide and his partner who is cross court to the ball should move closer to the center.

*My partner and I often go for the same lobbed ball. How can we avoid this?*

Talk a little bit to each other. Shout "Mine" or "Yours." Don't be afraid to talk with your partner. It can't hurt and it will be helpful.

*Is it better to lob or go down the center when our opponents are at the net with us?*

You shouldn't attempt a lob volley over your opponents' heads once in a hundred times. If you don't hit a lob volley perfectly, you will either knock it over the baseline or hit it so short your opponents can straighten up, smash it back, and you'll be eating fuzz.

You may not hit the ball exactly down the center but you have much more leeway than trying for a smaller area. In any event, you always stand a better chance of making a point in doubles if you keep the ball in play down the center. Try for a volley through the middle, because you are shooting into a larger area of the court or punch it straight at your closest opponent.

# 7.
# HOW TO PLAY THE BACKCOURT

*Where should I stand?*

Stand one or two feet behind the baseline about halfway between the singles sideline and the center stripe. You want to divide your opponents' possibilities in half and your responsibilities in half.

If a ball draws you a few steps inside the baseline and you are unable to continue to the net, you should retreat instantly behind the baseline again.

Many people hit the ball from in front of the baseline and stay there. When the ball is volleyed back deep into the court, it's at their feet because they were in no-man's land. That's a no-no. You should try never to be caught there. Either be behind the baseline or in front of the service line.

*What are my best possibilities from the back-court?*

You should try to keep your shots more or less in the middle of the court because that lessens your opponents' angle of return and does not open up your own court. It might also introduce a moment of indecision for your opponents as to who should play the ball.

The center theory of doubles has proved practical because if you keep hitting the ball down the

2 or 3 Feet Behind Baseline
After You Have Returned Serve and Cannot Get to Net

middle, your opponents are less likely to hit an angled volley which you cannot reach.

*Should I hit soft dropping balls when my opponents are at the net?*

If you're in the backcourt you should hit medium-speed shots, trying to keep the ball low and down the center. If one of your opponents is on the baseline, you should hit the ball to him as deep as possible. The depth will give you time to get to the net.

Don't slug. Some players get panicky or desperate when they're in the backcourt and their opponents are at net. When you hit a ball with all your might, the chances of keeping it in are slim, so don't hit so hard. Try for control rather than speed. This way at least your opponents will have to beat you; you won't beat yourself.

*What is the best way to handle a high bounce from behind the baseline?*

Good players will attempt a smash but most people should handle the ball as a regular forehand. If your opponents have control of the net, hit a high, deep lob which will give you time to recover. Unless they hit a great smash, you will be back in the point.

*Is it a good idea to remain in the backcourt?*

No. In doubles you want to spend as little time as possible in the backcourt. Most of the time one of you is at the net while the other is working to get to the net as soon as possible. Your constant thought must be for both of you to get to the net.

With two players at net, it is impossible for opponents to hit winners consistently from the backcourt.

*Why is it that after an extensive backcourt rally I am usually the first to hit the ball into the net?*

You probably aren't getting the racket back quickly enough on ground strokes or you are paying too much attention to the net man and not concentrating enough on watching the ball until you make contact with it.

Many players feel that if the ball is going back and forth too often, they have to do something to win the point outright. Try to out-steady your opponent and concentrate on the proper mechanics, not making a winning shot. Also try to work your way to the net. When rallying, be patient.

*During a cross-court rally my opponent hits a short ball to me and after I have returned it and gone to the net, he invariably lobs over my head which means my partner and I must run back. What am I doing wrong?*

You are probably not being aggressive enough when you get the short ball.

Think of yourself as a lion in the grass. When the short ball comes, you should pounce on it instead of caressing it. Be aggressive with your return and hit the ball deep, making it difficult for your opponent to hit a lob. Don't be afraid to miss a few because you are being aggressive; the overall results will be better.

If a defensive lob is hit over your head, you should remain at the net and duck down so your partner has his choice as to where to hit his smash. You aren't in the way. He should then work his way back to the net.

The only time you should retreat from the net is when your opponents have hit an offensive lob over your head which your partner should return as a defensive lob. Then you both should get behind your baseline in preparation to defend against an overhead smash.

*One of the group I play with has a chop stroke which gives me fits. What am I doing wrong that is giving me trouble with the return?*

A chop has a tendency to shoot or slide through faster than a flat- or top-spin ball. The under spin on a chop will make your return go lower.

You should prepare your racket earlier and aim the ball higher than normal, because the under spin will bring your shot down more quickly than normal.

*What about hitting drop shots?*

Drop shots are risky and should never be tried in doubles. If you're inside the baseline and can hit a drop shot, you're in just as good a position to hit a shot deep. If you misjudge the distance you're not in real trouble. But if you try a drop shot and misjudge, you can hit it too deep, too high, or miss it.

*What is my best defensive shot from the backcourt?*

There is only one: A good defensive lob. (See section on lobbing.)

*Why is it that when there is pressure on me in a backcourt rally I tend to slug or overhit the ball?*

Chances are when you are in trouble you take too big a swing at the ball. When pressed, you should be thinking of getting out of difficulty, so you should take a very controlled swing to be accurate. When the pressure is heaviest, that's the time to hit the ball coolly and with the best mechanics at your disposal.

Don't get excited and overplay your shots. When you have exchanged two or three hard shots, it's a good time to take a little speed off your next shot to maintain control. A common fault is trying to hit each shot on a given point harder than your previous shot.

# 8.
# HOW TO LOB

It seems to me that the lob is one of the misused and most misunderstood shots in tennis. It is not used nearly enough by many weekend players because, for some reason, they consider it a sissy shot. In reality it is one of the best weapons in the game.

There are two types of lobs—offensive and defensive. Their names describe their purposes.

An *offensive lob* should only be hit from inside the baseline, on a low trajectory, just high enough so your opponents can't jump and reach it and hopefully won't have time to run back and get the ball after it bounces.

## Offensive Lobs

*When should I use an offensive lob?*

Only when you are inside the baseline and when both of your opponents are at the net. If you feel they are crowding the net or if one man is making the common mistake of standing too close to the net, an offensive lob should be effective.

A good offensive lob will either win the point outright for you or get your opponents away from the net.

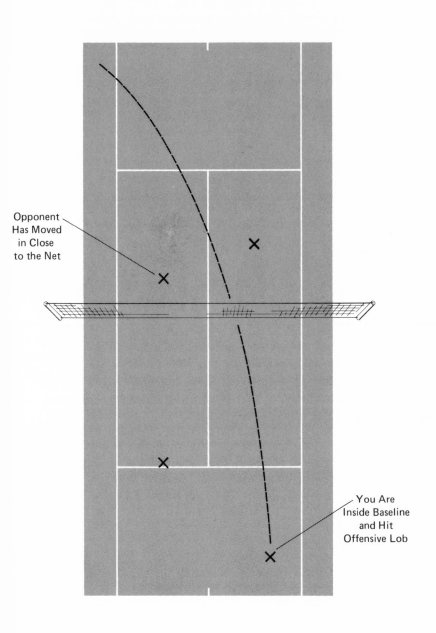

Opponent
Has Moved
in Close
to the Net

You Are
Inside Baseline
and Hit
Offensive Lob

*When should I not try an offensive lob?*

When you are behind the baseline you should not try to lob offensively because the ball must travel so far it is practically impossible to get it over an opponent's head and still keep it in court.

*Where is the best place to aim an offensive lob?*

An offensive lob over your opponent's backhand side is very difficult for him to handle.

If you lob into the middle of the court but hit a little to the right or left, it will still stay in the court. If you try to lob down an alley and mistime the shot, it can easily go out beyond the sideline.

Most people are better off trying to lob diagonally across court, however, because they will be hitting into the longest part of the court, thus giving themselves a better chance of keeping the ball in court.

*What kind of stroke should I use to make an offensive lob?*

Use a full stroke without quite as much backswing but a good follow-through. You don't need to take a big backswing because you're not trying to hit the ball really hard in terms of velocity but you are trying to make it travel a fair distance.

When many players lob they have a tendency to fall away from the ball. A lob should be a complete stroke and not a half stroke. When possible step into the shot just as though you are hitting a ground stroke.

*What should I do after I have lobbed offensively?*

If your opponents have to run back to get the lob, then you and your partner should run to the net and get into your volleying positions.

*Why is it so difficult for me to hit an offensive lob off my backhand?*

If you can hit a backhand return of service or a backhand passing shot there's no reason you can't hit an offensive lob properly off your backhand. It's basically the same swing, but on an upward trajectory.

You are probably not preparing the racket early enough, or are not watching the ball, or are not making a complete follow-through. You may also be falling away from the ball as you lob.

*What is the best way to return an offensive lob?*

Always try to get it in the air as an overhead smash. That way you will not give up your offensive position at the net.

When it's a low-trajectory ball you've given the net away if you run back and let it bounce, assuming you can get to it. Whenever you can reach a ball in the air, even if it stretches you out and you can't be really aggresssive with it, hit it and get back to the net.

*What if I have to run back to get the lob?*

In my estimation there's only one shot to hit then and that's a defensive lob. Stay behind the baseline until your opponents have returned the ball and then try to work your way back to the net.

Conceivably, all four of you could be behind the baseline at that stage and it will become a question of who hits the first short shot allowing the opposition to rush the net.

# Defensive Lobs

*When is a defensive lob used?*

When you are in trouble and want to buy time to recover from a difficult playing situation and when it is unlikely that, percentagewise, you will be able to get the ball past either of the opposing net men. The ball should be hit high and preferably deep into the court.

*What is the advantage of a defensive lob?*

It gives you and your partner time to get into the ideal defensive position and hopefully back on equal terms with your opponents. If you hit the ball very high and deep from behind the baseline, your opponent has to look at it for a long time which might make it more difficult for him to make a good smash. In any case you make your opponent beat you instead of you beating yourself by trying a low percentage shot from a poor court position.

*Should I rush to the net after making a defensive lob?*

No, because in all probability it will be returned as an overhead smash. The best position for you and your partner after one of you has hit a defensive lob is about three feet behind the baseline.

*Why is it that my defensive lobs always seem to land too shallow in the court?*

Chances are you are not making a complete stroke. It's very seldom that the average player hits a defensive lob past the baseline, so if you are lobbing short, it might be a good idea for you to say to yourself, "If anything I'm going to hit this lob over the baseline but I'm not going to hit it short." This will help you get more depth on your lobs.

You can take a full swing at the ball when making a defensive lob. Let's say the ball goes up in the air 40 feet and you have hit it from behind the baseline, which means it can travel the full length of the court which is 78 feet. That kind of distance requires a full stroke and the higher and deeper the ball goes, the more likely it will be difficult for your opponent to handle.

Beware of any existing wind, for a defensive lob will be greatly affected by the wind.

If a defensive lob is hit high, which means it will be well above the height of the fence, there might be more breeze up above. The ball is not traveling as fast as a ground stroke, which means it is more susceptible to wind.

If you have a cross wind, for example, you have to be aware of it because the wind will catch the ball and blow it around. If you have the wind behind you, you can't start the ball up in the air with the same depth because it will be blown deeper. Conversely, if the wind is in your face, you have to drive the ball into the wind more because it will be blown back somewhat.

### *How should I return a defensive lob?*

Under no circumstance do I recommend that you try to hit a defensive lob in the air. When your opponents have hit a defensive lob to you, let it bounce.

When the ball is coming down the first time it is traveling fast and falling almost straight down, so you are more likely to mistime and mishit the ball.

But after the ball bounces and comes down the second time, it is traveling more slowly. This makes it easier to time and hit.

Another reason for not hitting a defensive lob in the air is that by the time you can make contact with the ball your opponents have had all the time they need to get to their desired positions.

### *What can I do when playing against opponents who constantly return every ball as a lob?*

Take their offensive lobs in the air as a volley and continue to the net. Return their defensive lobs as overhead smashes after the ball has bounced.

Frequently when somebody lobs every return you will tend to lob back. In effect they have made you play their game and chances are you aren't going to lob as effectively as they do because they're accustomed to playing that way.

You have to be willing to be aggressive on overhead smashes when the opportunity is right. If you miss a couple, don't get cautious and go back to trying to out-lob them.

If they hit high lobs, don't be lazy and hit backhand returns. Get around the ball and take it on your forehand, going for depth, and then work your way back to the net because probably they are not coming to the net.

Don't get disgusted because that's what they hope you will do.

Be patient. As soon as you get a short ball, be the lion in the grass. Pounce on it.

*How can I follow a lob that has been hit up into the sun?*

Be aware of where the sun is when you start your match. Get on the side of the ball or get around it so that the sun is not shining into your eyes. If you are unable to look up into the glare, then let the ball bounce and take it on your forehand.

## CHECK LIST FOR LOBBING

A.   Am I watching the ball until impact?
B.   Am I making a complete stroke?
C.   Is my wrist firm?
D.   Did I lean into the ball?
E.   Was my racket prepared early enough?

# 9.
# MIXED
# DOUBLES

*I have noticed that in your tennis career you rarely played mixed doubles. Is there a reason for that?*

The main reason is that when I was playing amateur tennis, I felt men's singles and doubles were enough. Had I played mixed doubles there would have been times when I might have played a five-set singles match, a best of five-set men's doubles, and then late in the day I would have had to play two out of three sets of mixed doubles. I felt this would have helped tire me out for the more important singles and men's doubles events.

Also, I didn't like playing mixed doubles because I was never able to really take advantage of the girl on the other side of the net. I never felt as though I accomplished something by knocking a ball past a girl.

Now that my tennis playing is mostly confined to social matches, I enjoy playing mixed doubles because I can play for fun and not just to win. That philosophy, by the way, sometimes makes me a poor partner. I refuse to do the things that are necessary to play winning mixed doubles, that is, take advantage of my female opponent.

*What's the difference between playing mixed doubles socially and to win?*

As much difference as between night and day or, if you will, as between men and women.

*How should I play mixed doubles to win?*

If you're going to play mixed doubles for real, you must try to win at all costs and that means you must do all the things I dislike.

You must hit every ball you can at your female opponent. You have to try to dominate and crush her, even frighten her by hitting hard balls straight at her when she's at net. You have to serve hard to her and take advantage of her at every opportunity, which is neither fun nor chivalrous in my opinion.

Stay back on the baseline when your partner is receiving service from your female opponent because chances are the man on the opposite side will poach on her return. If you are behind the baseline you have a better chance to get his shot.

Once the ball is in play, get to the net as quickly as possible. You should then poach and put away every ball you can reach. If you want to win, you must cover 11/10 of the court.

If your partner has a weak backhand and she is serving into the ad court, try playing Australian style so the receiver is forced to hit to her forehand. But be certain she does not serve to the man's forehand because he can pull the ball down the line too easily.

When your partner is serving, she should do everything possible to get the first serve in deep without too much angle which opens up your court.

*How do you suggest I play mixed doubles for fun?*

If you're playing social tennis and want to have some fun and exercise, you should treat your female partner as you would a male of her ability. And you should treat the woman on the other side as you would a man of the same ability.

If you and the other man are better players than your female partners, I suggest you play the best game you can with emphasis on trying to keep the ball in play so everyone gets a chance at it. Try to make the tennis fun for the girls and you'll enjoy it, too. Let the girls hit some shots—don't just set the ball up to them but hit some where they can reach them. Don't serve so hard to them, and don't poach so much.

*What about husbands playing with their wives as partners?*

That's like husbands and wives playing bridge together. It usually doesn't work because they tend to take verbal liberties with one another that they would not take with another partner.

If the husband is the stronger player—which is frequently the case—he tends to be impatient when his wife makes bad shots and he starts giving her a lesson on the court which gets her up-tight. They end up fighting each other instead of their opponents. They don't have as much fun either.

*Have you any advice for husbands who do play with their wives?*

The best advice is for both to agree in advance that they are on the court to have fun. Neither one of them is going to give the other any harsh words or lessons. And they should encourage each other when they make good shots and encourage and console after bad ones.

Try to remember that your partner never misses a shot on purpose. Do you?

Of course it's easier to say this than do it, but that's the only way I think married partners can play together happily. At least it works that way when my wife and I are partners.

*How about playing opposite your wife?*

That depends on how competitive and serious she is about playing and winning.

It's never a good idea to embarrass a spouse in public with words and it's equally unwise to embarrass her on the court, especially since you probably know better than anyone else which shots she can't handle.

Before the match starts, you might say to your wife, "Look, we're on opposite sides of the net and this is a competitive match. You really can't ask for any quarter on the tennis court but remember, no matter who wins I love you and we're going home together!"

It certainly doesn't hurt to encourage your wife when she makes good shots even if they are at your expense. Have fun. It's only a game.

*What are some of the most common weaknesses of women as partners in mixed doubles?*

I don't know if they are weaknesses or common faults, but I have noticed over the years that most women have trouble in certain areas.

*98*

They usually stand too close to the net, making it easy to get lobs over them. I think that's because women are more frightened at net than men and seem to think there is protection in being closer to the net. That's a fallacy, however; a woman should play in the same position as a man when she's at net (see section on How to Play Net), so that she has more time to prepare for her volleys and to make it more difficult to lob over her head.

Surprisingly, many women poach too often probably because they are straining to appear helpful to their partner.

They try to hit the first serve too hard when, even if they get it in with all their strength, it probably won't cause the receiver any difficulty. Then, because they miss the first serve, they get rattled and nervous and tend to hit the second serve very softly to be sure they don't serve a double-fault.

Most women are not good on high volleys which is possibly because men are accustomed to sports which call for them to use their arms overhead while girls don't grow up throwing and catching footballs and baseballs.

They all hate a wide serve to them in the deuce court.

*What is the woman's obligation in mixed doubles?*

The same as the man's, but her ability to perform the obligation is lessened because most women are not as athletic or strong and fleet of foot as men. If she is playing to win, she should get her first serve in deep, return service cross court, and let her partner get every ball he can reach.

*What is the man's obligation in mixed doubles?*

To get to all the balls his pretty partner can't reach, to have fun, and to smile!

10.

# STRATEGY

*Is there a basic strategy to playing doubles?*

Yes. The basic strategy is to get both people to the net as quickly as possible. Unfortunately most weekend players do not work hard enough physically to get into the net position. They make a shot and then stay where they are instead of trying to move into the net. You must work hard to get into the proper position at net. Never stay in no-man's land.

Once at the net, you should hit the ball low to your opponents so they have to hit up to you. You're trying to make them hit up and you're trying to hit down.

As I have said so often in this book, you should work to get a better percentage of first serves in even if you sacrifice some speed. If you hit a pretty good deep serve with some spin, it will give you more time to get into the volleying position because the ball doesn't travel as fast and thus doesn't get back to you so quickly.

The harder you hit the ball the harder it may come back at you, but the longer your opponent has to wait before hitting the ball the more time you have to hustle to the net.

Let's say you hit a serve a little slower than normal to make certain of getting it in. You must still hustle to get into a good volleying position. Your opponents may knock the ball past you or your partner but you were still at least in position to make a good percentage play. It will work for you most of the time.

*What do you mean by a percentage play or playing percentages?*

It means you're hitting a lot of your best-type strokes and you're giving yourself the best chance of being successful.

Some examples of good percentage plays:

If your forehand cross-court shot is better than your forehand down the line, you should go cross court when you are under pressure because you are more likely to make it.

Hitting a spin serve as against a flat serve because you are more apt to get the spin serve in.

Volleying up the center of the court instead of near the sidelines because you are more apt to keep the ball in the court. Even if you mistime or mishit it, you're still okay, whereas if you try to go down an alley or close to a sideline, you are more likely to hit out.

Be aggressive with the ball when it's higher than the top of the net. If you're not in a position to do that, then try to get it down low to make them hit to you, or deep if at least one man is on the baseline.

Change of pace. Any variety is good because it's an added dimension and your opponents should never be certain just what you're going to do. For example, if you've hit three balls fairly hard at your opponents, take some speed off the next shot. Or if a man is at the baseline and you're rallying cross court, deuce court to deuce court, hit three or four hard shots and then hit a half lob and run in to net.

Know your strengths and your weaknesses. If your backhand is a weak stroke, run around it to take the ball on your forehand unless you put yourself in a difficult position on the court by doing so. If you're under pressure, don't try to hit your backhand down the line. Hit cross court.

If there's a wind blowing cross court, hit into the wind and don't go down the line with the wind.

If you're at the net and an opponent is at the baseline and the ball you are going to volley is below the top of the net, get it back deep and don't try to do a lot with it.

When you hit an overhead smash, hit the ball with a flat face and don't try to slice it. With a flat face you have the biggest area you can expose to the ball.

Aiming over the lowest part of the net because at the center you have six inches less to clear and the best chance of keeping the ball in court.

Hitting up the center of the court and not hitting wide-angled shots at your opponents, thus opening up too much of your court.

Hitting a defensive lob instead of trying to hit a ground stroke when you are several feet behind the baseline and both of your opponents are at the net.

Playing it safe is *not* a good percentage play when your opponents are a notch or two above you in ability. Just getting the ball back is not a winning tactic. You shouldn't go for broke and swing from the heels but you should try to make a decent shot. You may miss some but you'll win some too.

*Is there a psychology of winning?*

Yes, and I call it a positive attitude. Don't ever give your opponents the feeling that you're upset or worried or nervous and not in control. They may have the same attitude, too, which is fine. When you have two positive teams on the court who think they can win, it's going to be a tough match if both pairs are even in ability.

Self-control is very important. You can name people you know who blow their stacks and still win, but in general I have always felt that if I couldn't control my own emotions it would be impossible for me to control my opponent in any manner.

*While watching professionals play matches I am always amazed by their ability to anticipate where their opponents will return balls. Is there any way I can develop that kind of anticipation?*

There are two keys to anticipation.

The first is to recognize what type of shot you have hit to your opponents.

A good player knows where his opponents are most likely to return a ball because they have placed the ball in the court in such a position that they have eliminated some of the possibilities. They know from experience that their opponent can only make one or two possible returns from certain positions on the court. This ability has been refined after thousands of matches.

But you can do it, too. If you've hit a cross-court shot wide of the alley and your opponent has had to run wide, you know he is going to arrive to the ball at the very last second. That means he is going to be stretched out. Since he is getting to the ball late, he can't hit cross court. He either has to go down the line or lob. Since you have eliminated the cross-court shot as a possibility, you should move to cover a shot down the line and not get in so close to the net that he can lob over your head.

The second key to anticipation is knowing your opponent.

When I was a touring pro, I kept careful mental notes on the types of shots that my opponents liked and disliked. Over a period of time you learn a great deal about the people you play and can use this information to your advantage.

If I was meeting an opponent for the first time and knew nothing about him and had never had a chance to see him in action, I used the warm-up session to feel him out and find out what kind of shots he handled well or badly.

As a weekend player who probably comes in contact with the same group of people in match after match, you should know some of the weaknesses and strengths of your opponents.

Study your opposition before and during a match and you will find that regardless of how good they are, they have certain patterns of play which tell you what shots to avoid and what shots to use. For example, one of your opponents may not be able to hit a forehand down the line, so when you hit to his forehand, you should instantly cover the cross-court return.

Most weekend players have refined one or two shots that they like and use successfully. Be aware of their strengths and patterns and instantly start to cover the probable return.

If, for example, you know an opponent usually

hits his backhand cross court, then as soon as you hit to his backhand you try to get to the net before he has made contact with the ball. Then you make a head and shoulder fake toward the down-the-line shot so he sees some movement in that direction, but as soon as he begins his swing, you go cross court and wait for the ball because the percentages indicate that he is going to hit cross court.

*How should I treat a partner who constantly glares when I miss shots?*

We have all played doubles with a partner who tried to give us lessons throughout the match. Actually I don't believe there is anything wrong with a partner making suggestions. In fact, it's common practice in professional matches for partners to talk over their opponents' weaknesses and strengths. But that's not running each other's lives, nor do we get angry when a point is missed.

If you play with someone who insists on criticizing every shot and who scowls or glares at you every time you miss a shot, I suggest you look around for a new partner.

Many people make the terrible mistake of feeling that they have to win or the day has been a failure. I wonder why those people are playing in the first place. Most nonprofessionals play tennis for entertainment, a little exercise and some camaraderie. They're out there for fun and it shouldn't be vital that they win.

I believe my approach to golf is a good one. I'm a nine handicap and I've shot as low as 72 but basically I shoot around 80. My purpose in playing golf is to be with nice people and have some fun. I'm not on the course to make a living at it and I'm not there for someone to make a living off me. No matter what I do or what I shoot on Sunday, I'm going back to work on Monday, so I enjoy my golf no matter what I shoot.

*Unfortunately, I am also one of those people who gets upset with my partner when he misses shots. Is there anything I can do to correct this bad character trait?*

Realize that you are on the court to have some fun and exercise.

From my point of view, the worst thing you can do is to get angry with your partner. You don't help him by letting him know you're upset. All you do is make him a little more nervous or less confident, which means he is going to be less effective. You're only subverting your own cause.

I talk with my partner all the time, encouraging him when he makes good or bad shots. If he misses the easiest shot in the world and we lose my serve or the set, why should I be angry with him? He didn't do it on purpose and the next game or next day I might miss an equally important shot.

There's only one situation that might arise when I would be angry with my partner and that's if I thought he wasn't trying. Anytime there's more than one person on your side, you have to have teamwork and unity, common purpose and common understanding.

Never give your opponents any fuel for encouragement. I fed off opponents who got nervous or complained about balls or bickered with their partners, because I figured that was the time to try to split them wide open and thus win easily.

*Why is it that my partner and I are so frequently caught off guard when our opponents make an impossible or lucky return from one of our best shots?*

When the average player hits a ball that he considers good, he tends to think the point is over. Be ready at all times. Expect every ball to be returned until you see it bounce twice or hit the fence. That way, if your opponents make a lucky return and the ball comes back over the net, you're still prepared.

Don't ever quit. If your opponents don't put the sitter away and you can get it back and win the point, you will take some starch out of them.

*Is there any advantage to orally replaying and rehashing a match after losing it?*

Yes, and that's one of the advantages of losing occasionally. If you care about the game, you and your partner can analyze your mistakes and rehash your strategy so that the next time you play you are better prepared.

When you win, it's human nature to think you have played pretty well or you wouldn't have won, so you usually give it less thought. Losing a match can also spur you on and make you work harder.

*How can I handle calls I think are bad or un-
fair?*

Instead of stewing about a bad call for the next
three points and perhaps losing a match, you
should say to yourself, "Well, it was out. I thought
it was good but it was out." They call their side,
and you call yours.

Concentration is the name of the game and
you should not allow anything to interrupt it. If
you can maintain good concentration, you will
play better.

*How can I curb my bad temper during a match?*

The best way to curb your temper is to try your
best and keep your mouth shut.

If you realize why you're on the court, there's
no reason for you to be ill tempered. You're there
for fun and exercise and, win or lose, you're going
back to work the next day so what's the difference?

Realize that you're not a machine and that you
will make mistakes. For some reason a lot of
people think they play better than they actually
do. How can you possibly expect not to miss shots?
The best players in the world miss shots and they
practice every day and it's their livelihood. Since
it's not your way of life there's no excuse for
being a jerk about it when you lose.

*What should I do if I am the strongest player
of the group?*

One thing *not* to do is to be sloppy. If you're
the strongest player, then try to make the game

fun and interesting for the others. Practice your second serve and get it in where the opposing player can reach it. Don't put quite as much speed on the ball and try to keep it in play. This is also a good time to practice your timing: Hit the ball on the rise instead of letting it fall. Practice your strokes and fundamentals properly.

# GENERAL QUESTIONS

*I frequently have to sit out a set or two between matches and I never play well after the waiting period. Is there anything I can do?*

I don't think many people play well after having gotten hot and then stopping play, because in the interim period you begin to stiffen up a little bit and your muscles cool down and contract.

The best thing you can do is keep warm while you are off the court. Put on a sweater and perhaps wear warm-up pants.

If your next match is important, you should try to avoid sitting down while waiting. Walk around and perhaps jog in place or do some other light exercises.

Dress warmly to stay as hot as possible so your muscles don't cool off.

Don't eat and drink too much between matches. If you must eat, avoid heavy foods and iced drinks.

When you go back out on the court, keep on enough clothes so that you break a sweat as quickly as possible.

*I hear about crucial points during a match. What are they?*

It's difficult to define the crucial points, but obviously any time you have an ad on an opponent's serve, it's crucial, because if you win the point you get a service break. Conversely, when your opponents have the advantage on your service, it's crucial for them and you.

But most players have enough problems keeping the ball in play so all points are pretty important. Until you get so pooped you can't walk, you ought to try for every point.

Don't concern yourself with so-called crucial points. They all count.

*My partner is an A player and I am a C, but we always get beaten by a team of B's. Shouldn't we be able to beat them?*

In doubles you are only as good as your weaker link. Two medium players should beat a good player and a weak player because the medium players are good enough and the court is big enough to allow them to keep the ball away from the A player and take advantage of the C player.

The A player (your partner) is probably trying to hit outright winners each time he gets the ball, so he probably makes more mistakes than normally.

*Is it better to concentrate on proper form or getting the ball back over the net?*

In this book I speak to you in ideal terms. I tell you to get the racket back, turn sideways, and follow through. But when you're in a match, your opponents are trying to do all they can to keep you from these fundamentals.

So when you're trapped in the worst and most awkward position, forget about form. Think only about getting the racket back in the hitting position because then, though you're off balance, you still have a chance to swing forward and make a shot. It will help if you watch the ball too!

Utilize form and the fundamentals whenever you can, however, because that gives you a groove and you have a chance to improve and be a more consistently good player.

*Should the average weekend player take lessons?*

Definitely. There's a lot of room for improvement in most people's games, so why not try to improve on the fundamentals and increase your understanding of the game?

But if you have been playing for any length of time and are grooved in your strokes and habits, don't let anybody make major changes in your strokes this late in your tennis life.

If you try to make major changes, you will probably play worse and enjoy the game less.

Remember the old adage: "You can't teach an old dog new tricks." You can take a youngster who has not spent years ingraining bad habits and change them but he has a whole lifetime to change.

Instead of having a pro attempt to redo your entire game, I suggest you ask him to change some things here and there that might make you more effective with what you now have.

When you start taking lessons, it takes guts to stick with what you have learned and weather the bad period when nothing seems to work right. Unfortunately, too many people revert to their old habits under pressure and then the lessons were wasted because they didn't work at what they learned long enough to make it an instinctive part of their game.

*Do you advise playing with people who are much better?*

I think it's a mistake to get in a match over your head because it's too frustrating. You are trying too hard and are too conscious of making errors. Play with people as good as you are or maybe a little better but don't overmatch yourself. It's too discouraging and demoralizing.

On the other hand, if you accept the fact that the other players are too good for you, then you won't have any ego problem and you may learn from it.

*Where should the heel of the hand be on the racket?*

It should be down by the butt of the racket on every stroke. There is no advantage to choking up on the racket and there are many disadvantages. You want the maximum leverage and reach that you can get. The butt on the handle is to keep your hand from slipping off.

*Why do some tournament players I've seen rub their racket handle on the net cable between games?*

They want to scrape any oil from the handle of the racket, so it isn't slippery. When I was playing competitive tennis, one of the last things I did before a match was wash my hands with soap and water. I wouldn't shake hands with anybody on the way to the court because I didn't want to get his body oils on my hand.

*Should I go after a ball if I am uncertain whether it is going in or out?*

The rule of thumb even with a good player is to play the ball if there's any doubt.

If the ball is within your reach and you think you have a good play on it, then you should take it even if there is some doubt in your mind about whether it is going to be in or out.

On the other hand, if you are out of position and have no chance to make any kind of shot, let a doubtful ball go by and hope it goes out. If it falls in, you haven't lost much because you weren't going to be able to make a good shot anyway.

*Should I change sides with my partner after each set?*

You are allowed to but I don't recommend it. In all likelihood you are both playing the sides which you handle best. It's probably wiser to change your tactics.

*Is it all right to hold three balls in the hand when serving?*

Never hold three. You only get two serves so there's no sense in holding more than two balls.

Extra balls in your hand make it more difficult to properly use your hand on the throat of the racket.

*What is the best way to avoid getting tennis elbow?*

Avoid hitting balls hard until you are warmed up. Start gently, building up the pace, making certain you are warm before you attempt hard serves or overheads.

There's no question in my mind that a steel racket will help most players avoid tennis elbow because the racket absorbs much of the shock.

If I were going to teach tennis ten hours a day, I would use only a loosely strung steel racket because then I would have no shock at all thanks to the combination of steel and the suppleness of the strings. My choice of steel racket is the Wilson T2000 or T3000.

*How can I help alleviate tennis elbow?*

Soak your elbow in hot water for a few minutes before you start to play, thus speeding the warming-up process. Or rub a little ointment or liniment on your elbow. Keep your sweater on until you are really perspiring.

When you are finished playing, cover up, no matter how uncomfortable it is because you are hot and perspiring. And don't sit around in wet clothes.

If you have severe pain, consult your doctor. He will probably give you shots and suggest rest.

*Is there any way to avoid getting headaches after playing in the sun?*

Chances are you have not eaten enough before you play. If you haven't eaten for many hours before playing, you are likely to get dizzy or light-headed. Your body is like the engine of a car. It needs fuel. If I were to play a serious match at 1:00 P.M., I would eat a nutritional meal at 10:00 A.M.

*Do you recommend hitting with two hands on the racket?*

No. I don't object to children hitting the ball with two hands because the racket may be heavy for them and it may be the only way they can make the stroke in time. I don't recommend two-handed shots for adult players without infirmities, however, because your reach is not as great and you have to be quicker to cover the court.

*There are times when I seem to be constantly mishitting the ball. Is there any reason for that?*

You're probably not watching the ball or you're too late getting the racket ready, so you slap at the ball, causing mishits.

*What is the sweetest sound in the world?*

The hiss of air escaping from a new can of tennis balls as it is being opened!

# Rules for "Sudden Death" or the 12-Point Tie-Breaker

The 12-point tie-breaker system may be used in any set which reaches six games all. The winner of the tie-breaker and consequently the set (which is recorded as 7–6) is the team which wins seven of the first twelve points played or which, if the tie-breaker reaches six points all, wins an advantage of two points (example: 8–6 or 11–9 or 15–13).

The system of serving is this:

If player A (of team A and B) has just completed his serve and the score is six games all, then player C (of team C and D) remaining at the same end of the court shall serve to the right and left courts in normal sequence. Player B then serves to the right and left courts and player D to the right and left courts. Six of the twelve points have now been played and the players change ends.

Player A now serves twice (right and left courts). At this juncture eight points have been played and it is possible that the score could be 7–1, in which case the set is over.

Assuming seven points have not been won by either team, it is now player C's turn to serve to the right and left courts and then player B serves two points.

At the conclusion of the twelve points, if neither team has won seven points, the player whose turn it is to serve (in this case player D) will serve one serve to the right court. Then player A will serve to the right court.

If neither team wins both points, then player C will serve to the left court and player A will serve to the left court. Again, if neither team has won the two points, players B and D will each serve once to the right court.

At this point, if the score is 9 all, the teams will change ends and each player will alternately serve to different sides. If the tie-breaker continues beyond 9 all, the teams change ends after every 6 points until one team has a 2-point advantage.

A somewhat similar 9-point sudden-death system is also sometimes used. But most players prefer the 12-point system. There are variations of the 12-point tie-breaker described above.

# GLOSSARY

ACE. A serve the receiver is unable to touch with his racket.

AD. Abbreviation for the word "advantage."

AD COURT. The second court served into, sometimes called the backhand or left court.

AD-IN. A scorekeeping term meaning the server has the advantage in a given game.

AD-OUT. The receiver has the advantage.

ALLEY. Area between the singles sideline or inside line and the doubles sideline or the outside line of the court.

AMERICAN TWIST. A serve which bounces higher and kicks off to the left of the receiver. The serve has part top spin and part side spin.

ANGLED VOLLEY. A volley hit diagonally across the court almost parallel to the net.

APPROACH SHOT. The ball hit as a player is approaching the net.

AUSTRALIAN FORMATION. A formation used by the serving team in doubles.

BACKCOURT. The area around the baseline.

BACK SPIN. A ball undercut so it rotates backward. Also called under spin.

BACKSWING. Taking the racket back in preparation for any stroke.

BASELINE. Back line at either end of the court.

BLOCKING. A very short punch at the ball taken with very little backswing, using the speed of the ball to get it back.

BREAK. When you win the other person's serve.

BYE. When there are not enough players in a tournament, certain players go through to the next round without playing an opponent.

CANNONBALL. A flat hard serve.

"CATCH HIM LEANING." You have influenced an opponent to lean in a certain direction to protect an area and then you hit in the opposite direction.

CENTER SERVICE LINE. Line up the middle of the court.

CENTER STRIPE. The small perpendicular line in the middle of the baseline. The server stands to the right or left of it depending on which court he is serving into.

CHIP. A softly hit ball with under spin.

CHOP. A ball hit with back spin.

CONTINENTAL GRIP. Refers only to a forehand grip. The hand is turned well over on the top of the racket in much the same position as for an orthodox backhand.

CROSS-COURT SHOT. A ball hit diagonally across the court.


DEFAULT. To lose a match by failing to show up.

DEFENSIVE LOB. High trajectory lob designed to give yourself time to recover and get back into position.

DEUCE. A score of 40–40 is deuce. A score of 30 all is not deuce.

DEUCE COURT. The right-hand court or the first court served into or the forehand court.

DINK SHOT. A softly hit ball which barely clears the net and drops at the opponent's feet.

DOUBLE-FAULT. Failure to get either of two serves into the court.

DOUBLES SIDELINE. Outside sidelines of the court.

DOWN THE LINE. A ball hit parallel to the sidelines.

DRAW. List of names drawn from a hat for a tournament indicating which players play each other.

DROP SHOT. A ball hit gently with under spin that lands just beyond the net.

DROP VOLLEY. A ball caught in the air which is dropped just over the net.


EASTERN GRIP. When the racket head is perpendicular to the ground and you shake hands with the handle. The hand is rotated for a backhand grip ¼ turn over the top.

FAKING. A feint designed to make your opponents believe you are going to change your position.

FAST COURT. A surface which causes the ball to bounce quickly.

FAULT. A service which does not go in the court.

FINALS. The last two players or teams remaining in a tournament.

FLOATER. A ball hit softly and high over the net.

FOLLOW-THROUGH. Continuation of the stroke after the ball has been hit.

FORCING SHOT. A ball hit with pace, giving an opponent a minimum of time to reach it.

FORECOURT. The area between the net and the service line.

FOREHAND COURT. Same as the deuce court.

GAME. One particular game, your service game or your opponent's.

GRAND SLAM. When a player wins the four major singles championships of the world in the same year: Australian National Championships, French National Championships, Wimbledon, and the U.S. National Championships. Only two men have accomplished this: Don Budge in 1938 and Rod Laver in 1962 and 1969.

GROUND STROKE. A ball hit forehand or backhand after it has bounced.

HALF VOLLEY. A ball hit immediately after it bounces, when you are playing at net.

HEAVY BALL. A ball which feels heavy when it makes contact with the racket.

HOLD SERVE. To win your serve.

"KEEPING HIM HONEST." Term used when a ball is hit down the net man's alley after he has poached a few times.

KICK SERVE. Top-spin, side-spin serve like the American Twist.

LADDER. A challenge system of competition in which any number of players are listed on a chart set up like the steps of a ladder. Any player can challenge either of the next two above him, and if the challenger wins, they change positions.

LET. A service which hits the top of the net but lands in the court and is replayed without penalty. Sometimes improperly called "net."

LINESMAN. An official who determines whether a ball lands in or outside the line he is calling.

LOB. A ball hit up into the air.

LOVE. Zero!

MATCH. A competition between players or teams that consists of a predetermined number of sets or games.

MATCH POINT. The last point needed to win a match.

NET BALL. Any shot after the serve that touches the net but lands in play.

NETCORD. A shot hit into the tape at the top of the net which rolls over into the opposite side.

NET GAME. The way a person plays when he is at the net. Includes volleys and overhead smashes.

NO-MAN'S LAND. Area between the baseline and service line.

OFFENSIVE LOB. A low-trajectory lob.

ON SERVE. No one has a service break.

OPEN FACE. Tilting the face of the racket back so it faces upward.

OVERHEAD. A ball returned from above your head.

OVER SPIN. The same as top spin. The ball rotates forward, or over the top.

PACE. The speed of the ball.

PASSING SHOT. An attempt to hit the ball past the man at net.

PLACEMENT. Any shot that an opponent cannot touch.

POACH. Moving into a partner's area to intercept an opponent's return.

PUT AWAY. A ball that is not touched by an opponent.

RALLY. The ball goes back and forth several times before the point is won.

RECEIVER. The player who receives the serve.

REFEREE. The man who runs a tournament and makes all the decisions.

RETRIEVER. A player who consistently gets the balls back.

ROUND ROBIN. A tournament in which every player or every team plays every other player or team.

RUSHING THE NET. The player tries to get to the net as quickly as possible.

SCISSORS. Name for a cross-over tactic in doubles in which the net man and the man in the backcourt quickly cross over to change positions.

SEEDING. The process by which top-ranked players are separated in a draw of a tournament so there is no way the number-one player and number-two player can meet until the final round.

SEMIFINALS. The four singles players or doubles teams remaining in a tournament in the round before the finals.

SERVE. A ball hit from behind the baseline to start a point.

SERVER. The player who puts the ball into play.

SERVICE-BREAK. Winning the opponent's serve.

SERVICE LINE. The lines running across the court parallel to the baseline on each side, the line in the center running parallel to the sidelines, and the sidelines.

SET. The unit of scoring. The first team to win six games with at least a two-game advantage wins the set.

SET POINT. The last point needed to win a set.

SIDELINES. The left and right boundaries of the playing area.

SITTER. A ball which is soft and easy to put away.

SLICE. Serve hit with side spin, like a curve in baseball.

SLOW COURT. A surface on which the ball bounces slowly and high.

SMASH. Same as an overhead.

SPIN. Rotating motion of the ball.

SPIN SERVE. An American Twist serve.

STOP VOLLEY. A ball which has been volleyed and drops over and near to the net.

STRINGS. The gut or nylon in the racket.

SWEET SPOT. The center of the racket head and therefore the center of the section of strings that strikes the ball.

SUDDEN DEATH. The new scoring system whereby when the players get to six games apiece they either play a 9- or 12-point tie-breaker and automatically end the set. (See Rules of Sudden Death Scoring in the Rules Section.)

TOP-SPIN LOB. A lob hit with a lot of top spin so it will go over a player's head and drop quickly into the court.

TOSS. The act of putting the ball up in the air when serving.

TRAMWAY. English term for the doubles alley.

TWO-HANDED SHOT. Any stroke in which the player uses two hands on the racket when he makes contact with the ball.

UNDERHAND. A serve hit from below the waist.

UNDER SPIN. The opposite of top spin. Same as back spin.

UMPIRE. The man who sits in the high chair at matches and calls out the score.

USLTA. The United States Lawn Tennis Association; the organization which governs amateur tennis in America.

VOLLEY. A ball hit in the air from either side of the body.

WESTERN GRIP. A method of gripping the racket. The hand goes well underneath the grip on the racket handle.

WRISTY. Hitting a ball using lots of wrist.

WRONG FOOT. A ball hit to a player's previous position so that he is caught running in the wrong direction.